FOR THE LOVE OF
DACHSHUNDS

FOR THE LOVE OF
DACHSHUNDS

ROBERT HUTCHINSON

BROWNTROUT PUBLISHERS
SAN FRANCISCO

Library of Congress Cataloging-in-Publication Data

Hutchinson, Robert, 1951-
  For the love of dachshunds / Robert Hutchinson.
    p. cm. — (For the love of)
  Summary: "Text investigates the conformation, genetics, and breed history of the Dachshund. Includes over 100 full-color photographs"—Provided by publisher.
  Includes index.
  ISBN 1-56313-903-0 (hardcover : alk. paper)
  1. Dachshunds. I. Title. II. Series.

SF429.D25H87 2004
636.753'8—dc22

2004027244

Published by BrownTrout Publishers, Inc.
P.O. Box 280070, San Francisco, CA 94128-0070 U.S.A.
800-777-7812
www.browntrout.com

CONTENTS

**L**ong, low, and tubular —there's no mistaking a Dachshund at any distance. This German breed's outlandish build has long inspired the wurst jokes. No sooner had the first Dachshunds stepped off the boat in America in the company of German émigrés displaced by the crushing of the 1848 Revolution than they found themselves the butts of dockside wags, who variously hailed them as *wiener dogs, German sausage dogs,* and *frankfurter dogs.*

American folk humorists of the later nineteenth century flipped the quip and renamed the frankfurter the *hot dog.* The catalyst for this gag was an enterprising Bavarian immigrant named Anton Ludwig Feuchtwanger, who had secured a sausage vending concession at the 1893 World's Columbia Exposition in Chicago. One day in May, Feuchtwanger was passing out the customary white gloves for the protection of the fingers of his hot wiener customers when he had a brainstorm worthy of George Westinghouse: Why not encase the hot wieners in elongated bread rolls and forget the stupid gloves!

Over the next six months, millions of visitors to the Exposition were subjected to Feuchtwanger's stentorian voice hawking his brilliant invention as they strolled down the Midway Plaisance: "Red hot dachshund sausages!" Fairgoers by droves queued up and ordered "hot dachs." Before that festive summer of '93 was over, the descanting cry of " Hot dogs!" had risen for the first time over an American ballpark—the nearby Congress Street Grounds, home of the legendary Chicago White Stockings.

The notion of sinking one's teeth into a steaming Dachshund smothered in mustard and onions strikes us as crudely funny because it violates the taboo in Western cultures against eating dog. As the long-suffering subject of this edacious word play, the Dachshund may be credited with saving the frankfurter industry in the United States during the passionately anti-German days of World War I—when *sauerkraut* was de-Germanized to *liberty cabbage*; when *German Shepherd Dog* was Frenchified to *Alsatian*; and when *frankfurters*, tainted with the odor of Teutonic treason, were Americanized to *hot dogs.*

Notwithstanding its patriotic service as the logos of the eucharistic *hot dog* of the American ballpark, the Dachshund was cruelly hounded for its German name and ancestry after the sinking of the *Lusitania.* It spelled double trouble for expatriate

Everyone Loves a Wiener

Dachshunds that photographs and cartoons of Kaiser Wilhelm in the American and British press commonly showed the monocled martinet attended by an imperial entourage of Dachshunds. The hasty anglicizations of *Dachshund* to *Badger Dog* in the United States and to *Badger*

Hound in Britain failed to curb the zeal of self-appointed Bosch-bashers and spy-catchers, who did not remit the volleys of kicks, curses, and stones reserved for such Dachshunds and their fifth-columnist owners as dared venture outdoors together.

Under such duress, the Dachshund population of the Allied world crashed during the Great War. In Chicago, a frightened breeder was reported to have shot every Dachshund in his kennel rather than face further contumely. In 1913, 217 Dachshunds were registered in Britain; in 1919, none. In the United States, the Dachshund went from being one of the ten most numerous breeds at Westminster in 1913 to being represented by only 12 lone survivors in 1919.

With the dismantling of the anti-German propaganda machines after the German surrender, however, anti-German hysteria quickly dissipated and the Dachshund enjoyed a complete rehabilitation in America and Britain. High-quality studs from currency-strapped Germany flooded the British market and replenished its decimated kennel stock. Exports from the revitalized British kennels shortly thereafter streamed on to the United States.

In 1923, the Dachshund's proper name was restored in the United States and the breed's registration numbers began a steady climb. By 1930, the Dachshund had reached the 28th rank of breed popularity in terms of American Kennel Club (AKC) registrations. By 1938, the Dachshund had climbed all the way to fourth place. Neither was the popularity of the Dachshund battered during the Second World War as it had been during the First—largely because the ideological context of the later war led the Allied propaganda machines to target less the evil character of the whole German race than the racist state imposed on Germany by evil individuals.

The Dachshund has ever since maintained its place amongst the top ten breeds in America. In 2003, its 39,473 new AKC registrations qualified the Dachshund as the fifth most popular breed in the United States. Atop the winners' dais, the *weeny dog* stands taller than a hundred breeds of greater stature. Also serving to keep the Dachshund in the public eye have been the intellectual efforts of American folk-humorists of the twentieth century, who have squeezed new boudinage out of the old wurst farce by re-renaming the Dachshund the *hot dog dog*—after the food article that had itself been renamed after the Dachshund.

It is dreadful to contemplate what links might be added to this chain of self-referential humor in the twenty-first century. Will the frankfurter be re-renamed the *hot hot dog dog*? And then will the Dachshund be re-re-renamed the *hot hot dog dog dog*? And then will the frankfurter be re-re-renamed...? Enough already! You want to teckel me to death? There is such a thing as stretching a joke too far, you know.

Unlike its body, however, the character of the Dachshund affords no material for the great wits of our age. That character—courageous, strong-willed, tenacious, independent, feisty, loyal—commands universal respect and admiration. A short selection from the long roster of famous Dachshund owners of the last century-and-a-half will suffice to illustrate the high esteem in which this low breed's character has always been held: Queen Victoria and Prince Albert, Matthew Arnold, Edward VII, Kaiser Wilhelm II, Pablo Picasso, Noël Coward, William Randolph Hearst, Adolphe Menjou, Errol Flynn, Carole Lombard and Clark Gable, John Wayne, Andy Warhol, and Jerry Dunn.

Jerry Dunn? Although this name is the least famous on the list, its owner ranks first as an authority on the Dachshund's indomitable character. Mr. Dunn is a 70-year-old resident of Minden, Louisiana, who set off across his lawn on the morning of November 20, 1998, to pick up his newspaper. Although he had noticed a big deer standing on the edge of the lawn, Mr. Dunn gave it no heed as he stooped over the morning headlines. At that moment, the stag charged and gored him with its antlers. As Mr. Dunn twisted in bloody agony on the buck's pounding rack, his Dachshund—Baxter—galloped to the rescue. "My little old weeny dog came round the house barking and chased the deer and the deer chased the dog," said Mr. Dunn from his hospital bed, crediting Baxter with having saved him from a ridiculous death.

How did such a big strong spirit as Baxter's come to lodge in such a zany little body? This paradox has a fascinating functional explanation. Once you know the explanation, you can no longer see anything comical in the Dachshund's body. To the contrary, you can only marvel at its singular stern beauty.

The form of the Dachshund follows its original function in Germany as a highly specialized underground hunter. The specialty is announced in the very name of the breed: *Dachs* means "badger" in German; *Hund* means "dog" (not "hound"). (In fact, the more common name for the Dachshund in its country

of origin is *Teckel*—the Bavarian-Austrian dialectal form of *Dachshund*, formed by Franconian soundshift of initial Germanic *d-* to *t-* and substitution of the final syllable by Bavarian diminutive *-el*. The allophonic Low German variants of *Teckel* are *Dackel*, *Dachel*, and *Dachsel* . These are simply fond diminutive forms of *Dachshund*—just as *Scottie* is of *Scottish Terrier*—except that *Dackel* carries the secondary colloquial meaning of "idiot" or "numbskull".) The Dachshund was developed by the foresters of the grand estates of the German aristocracy in the eighteenth and nineteenth centuries for a precise function: to go down the burrows of badgers and outface their denizens.

The Eurasian badger (*Meles meles*) is a fossorial omnivore. Besides acorns, berries, seeds, tubers, and

mushrooms, it gobbles carrion, birds, reptiles, frogs, and small mammals. The Eurasian badger especially relishes rodents and rabbits, whose little burrows it locates by the tiny scuttlings and squeakings from within and then plows up with a few powerful strokes of the long, non-retractile claws of its short, muscular forelegs.

Equally efficient at excavating its own big burrow, the badger digs a tunnel with an elliptical cross-section just big enough to pass its broad oval trunk. The Eurasian badger makes its burrow a foot high by two feet wide in order to accommodate its forty-pound wedge-shaped bulk (double that of either the American badger or the Standard Dachshund). This tunnel bores some fifty feet into the earth before terminating in a four-foot-diameter den as much as nine feet beneath the surface. It is down this long narrow tube that the Dachshund—the Badger Dog—was designed to cram himself with all the wacky gusto of a hot-dogging spelunker.

In full jocular title, then, the Dachshund might well be called a *hot diggety dog*. The breed was developed to crawl and dig to the end of a badger burrow and hold at bay whatever quarry might be immured in the den. The occupant might be the industrious badger himself—or perhaps an opportunistic fox who jumped the claim.

Now, it is not Badger's custom—contrary to his mild-mannered representation in *The Wind in the Willows*—to feign delight at an unsolicited visit to his private quarters. Indeed, wholesale unpleasantness may be depended to erupt upon the threshold of the chamber. The Dachshund plugs the exit with his rear end while engaging the enraged homeowner fang-and-claw. In the total darkness of the den, the Dachshund must—like a blindfolded Ninja warrior—rely exclusively on the acuity of his extravisual senses.

The Dachshund is now required to hold its quarry at bay until the human hunter monitoring topside

can dig down for the kill. But the human hunter cannot know where to apply his shovel unless the Dachshund communicates his buried coordinates. To this end, the embattled Dachshund gives his master "tongue" (*Laut*)—that is, he bays repeatedly and loudly enough to be heard through as much as nine feet of soil. Ideally, the Dachshund's master hears his *Laut*, digs down, and dispatches the vermin. Should his master fail to come within earshot, however, the Dachshund himself must carry the fight to its fatal conclusion.

Highly specialized predators tend to mimic advantageous features of their prey. On the savanna, for example, the cheetah has evolved long legs, low body fat, and keen sight to match those of the gazelle that it pursues. By like token, to hunt badger underground, the Dachshund has been supplied by its original breeders with many of the badger's characteristics: big chest; short legs; keen nose and ears; belligerence; tenacity.

The Dachshund's chest resembles that of the badger in being large, long, broadly oval, strongly ribbed, prominently keeled, and capacious. Robust chest dimensions are necessary in order to accommodate correspondingly large heart and lungs. Dachshund and badger alike need voluminous respiratory organs to prosecute, within the suffocating confines of a narrow burrow, their arduous work of crawling, digging, fighting, and—in the case of the Dachshund—yelling.

Both the Dachshund and the badger have to have big muscular chests for their underground exertions—but they also have to be able to fit down a badger's foot-high burrow. The simultaneous requirements of big chest and low stature together constrain the length and articulation of the legs. Both Dachshund and badger have short legs, although the Dachshund's are somewhat longer. The Dachshund needs the higher clearance for its aboveground approach work. The German rule is that the Dachshund's clearance must be no less than one-third the height to the withers. The English and American standards—catering more to beauty than performance—permit as low as one-quarter clearance.

To maneuver and dig through a badger's burrow, the Dachshund's legs must be strong. But how can its forelegs be shortened without sacrificing strength? The shortening of the Dachshund's foreleg has been won primarily from its forearm (radius and ulna). Although the Dachshund's forearm is thick, it is less than half the length of the upper arm (humerus)—whereas, in most dog breeds, the forearm is longer than the upper arm. By contrast, the well-angulated upper arm and shoulder blade (scapula) of the Dachshund are of normal size, thereby providing ample area for the heavy muscle attachments that endow the legs with strength.

The Dachshund and the badger both have amazingly acute senses of smell and hearing. The badger needs them to locate its rodent prey as they tiptoe underground in their little burrows. The Dachshund—whose remarkably sensitive nose is thought to derive from an early infusion of bloodhound (perhaps the pointy-muzzled *Schweisshund*)—needs keen extravisual senses in order to track a badger's foraging path and then take on the burly badger in its lightless den.

It must be allowed, however, that the Dachshund is rarely called upon to exercise more than a fraction of its olfactory faculty in order to smell out a badger. So rank an odor continually leaks from the badger's anal glands that the phrase, "stinking like a badger" ("*puant comme un taisson*"), has long been employed as the standard intensive idiom for "smelly" by the French. To disguise himself as a badger, therefore, the cunning Dachshund rolls in the badger's outside dung pit before venturing down the burrow. (The fragrant vestige of this behavioral adaptation in modern pet Dachshunds is all too familiar to many a bemused owner.)

When it comes to the clinch, the Eurasian badger

enjoys two advantages: it is almost twice as big as the original Standard Size (*Normalgrösse*) of the Dachshund; and it wields terrific Freddy Kruger-like foreclaws with the insensate ferocity of a University of Wisconsin red-dogger. On the downside, the badger is poky and short-necked. The Dachshund's countervailing weapon is its long, strong jaws that it can thrust and retract with a flick of its long, flexible neck.

To hold its own against an adult Eurasian badger in its subterranean bunker, the traditional working Dachshund could scarcely afford to weigh less than 20 lb. In the utterly different subaerial environment of the twentieth-century showring, the Dachshund breed has undergone downsizing and subdivision into a untidy multiplicity of classes based on systems of size and coat-type criteria which vary by country. Three competing systems of standard Dachshund breed classification are variously observed around the world: the German, British, and North American. Within the union of countries recognizing a given standard, all interbreeding across classes specified in that standard is forbidden.

Excepting national Dachshund clubs in the Anglophone world (most notably those of Great Britain and North America) and certain maverick clubs elsewhere (most notably the *Internationaler Dackel-Club Gergweis e.V.* based in Germany), Dachshund clubs throughout the world unanimously consent under the conventions of the *Fédération Cynologique Internationale* (FCI) to be governed by the German Teckel Club Standard (*Deutscher Teckelklub Rassestandard*: adopted in Stuttgart, 1925; amended 1946), inasmuch as the DTK qualifies as the parent club in the breed's country of origin.

The current DTK/FCI Standard recognizes three official size classes of Teckel, each to be separately bred and shown: *Normalgros, Zwerg,* and *Kaninchen.* To be classified *Normalgros* ("Standard"), a Dachshund may not weigh more than 9 kg (19.8 lb); and, ideally, should weigh 6.5-7 kg (14.3-15.4 lb). To be considered a *Zwerg* or "Dwarf", a Dachshund may not at 18 months weigh more than 4 kg (8.8 lb), nor may its chest circumference exceed 35 cm (13.8 in). Lastly, the *Kaninchen* ("Rabbit") may not at 18 months weigh more than 3.5 kg (7.7 lb), nor may its chest circumference exceed 30 cm (11.8 in). In German practice, however, scales are not consulted in the ring; and the chest circumference of an individual Dachshund is considered to have been unalterably established after a single certified measurement.

The DTK used to recognize other size classes at either extremity of the current range. Until 1947, the DTK Standard distinguished two size classes at the upper end in place of the current *Normalgros* size class: *Schwergewicht* ("Heavyweight") and *Leichtgewicht* ("Lightweight"), which were respectively heavier than and lighter than 7 kg (15.4 lb) for males and 6.5 kg (14.3 lb) for females. Prior to 1912, yet more confusingly, *Schwergewicht* referred to a class over 10 kg (22 lb) that ranged in practice up to 16 kg (35 lb). The DTK's withdrawal of recognition from this 22-35 lb class of Dachshunds in 1912 merely formalized a *fait accompli*: namely, the desuetude in Germany since the end of the nineteenth century of the practice of putting Dachshunds to the heavyweight business of badger-hunting.

In former times, the DTK used also to recognize a different set of classes at the lower end of the size range. Between 1902 and 1912, the DTK Standard recognized only one miniature class, the *Kaninchenteckel*—a catch-all for Dachshunds smaller than 5 kg. Thereafter, the DTK Standard was amended to subdivide the *Kaninchenteckel* class into a three separate classes: 1) *Kaninchenteckel,* a miniature Dachshund weighing more than 4 kg; 2) *Zwergteckel,* a miniature Dachshund weighing less than 4 kg; and 3) *Kaninchenhund,* any extremely short-legged hybrid dog of less than 4 kg engendered by crossing a

Dachshund of *Leichtgewicht* class with a representative of any toy breed. By 1935, the DTK had eliminated both the bastard *Kaninchenhund* class and the *Kaninchenteckel* class as formerly defined (i.e., heavier than 4 kg)—instead reassigning the name *Kaninchen* to a new sub-3.5 kg miniature Dachshund size class.

Although the modern DTK Standard has drastically simplified the old DTK size system to only three classes, the systems of the Anglophone clubs are simpler still. The Standard of the Dachshund Club/Kennel Club (DC/KC) of Great Britain—generally imitated by the standards of current (e.g., Canada) and former (e.g., South Africa) Commonwealth national breed clubs—recognizes only two size classes (to be bred and shown separately): *Standard* and *Miniature*. By contrast to the DTK/FCI Standard, the DC/KC Standard defines its two size classes by reference only to "ideal weights", without stipulating limiting weights or circumferences. Both are significantly heavier than their nearest German counterparts.

The DC/KC Standard recommends that the ideal weight of its Standard Dachshunds be 20-26 lb. Yet, as a matter of British practice, scales are not resorted to in Standard Dachshund competition and judges tend to reward bigger size. Many winners (especially in the Standard Smooth class) not only exceed 26 lb but even tip 30 lb. Few Standard winners in Britain these days weigh less than 23 lb. The weight range of the heavier British size class is therefore displaced about 10 lb above the weight range of the heaviest German size class (*Normalgross*).

In like manner, the DC/KC Standard recommends that the ideal weight of its Miniature Dachshunds be 10 lb. Although the Standard enjoins judges of Miniature competition (in which scales are routinely used) not to award prizes to animals over 11 lb, it does not prohibit such animals being shown or bred in that class. The maximum desirable weight of the lighter British size class is therefore 2 lb heavier than the maximum allowable weight of the intermediate German size class (*Zwerg*).

On the face of it, the simplest of all size systems is the American, insofar as the Standard of the Dachshund Club of America/American Kennel Club (DCA/AKC) declares that it does not classify Standard and Miniature Dachshunds as separate varieties. This disclaimer, however, turns out to be an anachronistic vestige of an old controversy that raged in the 1950s—before Miniature varieties had stabilized sufficiently to allow breeders to dispense with periodic outcrossing to Standards.

Rather absurdly, the paragraph of the DCA/AKC Standard that starts by doing reverence to the dead letter of unitary size classification ends by actually imposing a British-style two-tier system of Standard and Miniature weight classes that are to be separately bred and shown. The DCA/AKC Standard states non-prescriptively that Standard Dachshunds "usually" weigh between 16 and 32 lb; but prescribes that Miniature Dachshunds must weigh less than 11 lb.

Whereas Dachshund size-classes vary in number and definition from country to country, Dachshund coat-type classes are everywhere the same. In all countries, each 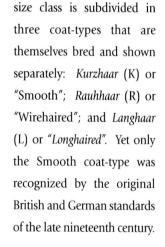 size class is subdivided in three coat-types that are themselves bred and shown separately: *Kurzhaar* (K) or "Smooth"; *Rauhhaar* (R) or "Wirehaired"; and *Langhaar* (L) or *"Longhaired"*. Yet only the Smooth coat-type was recognized by the original British and German standards of the late nineteenth century.

Wirehaired and Longhaired Dachshunds—the products of outcrossing Smooth Dachshunds respectively to terriers (definitely Dandie Dinmont Terriers; possibly Skye Terriers, Wirehaired Fox Terriers, and Wirehaired Pinschers also) and to spaniels (definitely *Wachtelhunde*, a.k.a. German Spaniels; possibly English Cocker Spaniels also)—were not

systematically bred (except perhaps in certain crown kennels such as that of Duke Ernest II of Saxe-Coburg-Gotha, brother of Prince Albert, consort of Queen Victoria) until the 1880s and were seldom seen in Germany until 1900. Not until 1915 did the DTK start to record the coat-type of a Dachshund in its registration (by means of the device adopted that year of affixing *K*, *R*, or *L* to its studbook registration number).

Several war-torn decades intervened before the non-Smooth Dachshund coat-types secured beach-heads in England and America. Wirehaired and Longhaired Dachshunds were not imported and bred under organized auspices in Britain until the late 1920s and '30s; nor in the United States until the 1930s and '40s. Although the popularity of Wires and Longhairs

has been surging in Britain and America in recent decades, they have not yet displaced the Smooths in the Anglophone world as utterly as they have in Germany.

Wires—representing three-quarters of total DTK registrations—are far and away the most popular variety of Dachshund in Germany today. Longhairs account for another fifth; whereas Smooths have dwindled to only a twentieth of the DTK total. In Britain, by contrast, Longhairs are most popular, with almost half the total registrations; Smooths and Wires split the difference about equally. The popularity rankings of the Dachshund coat-type classes vary not only by country but also by size-class within a country. In Britain, for example, Standard Smooths are more popular than Standard Wires but Miniature Wires are more popular than Miniature Smooths.

Under any given Dachshund breed standard, the number of closed classes within which all Dachshunds must be bred and shown equals the number of size-classes multiplied by the number of coat-type classes. In countries governed by the DTK/FCI Standard, therefore, Dachshunds are bred and shown in nine mutually exclusive classes; in countries governed or influenced by the DC/KC Standard, six classes; and in countries governed or influenced by the DCA/AKC Standard, six classes (in strict terms, three "classes" plus three "class divisions"). Since none of these classes is identically defined in any two systems, it follows that twenty-one reproductively closed classes of Dachshunds are presently established world-wide.

As we have seen, the proliferation of these many sub-domains of genetic closure within the Dachshund breed is a quite recent development. Derivation from recent common ancestors has operated in tandem with unified conformation requirements in the breed standards to guarantee a high degree of genetic kinship amongst the many modern varieties of Dachshund. The next chapter surveys the common ground in the genetics of the Dachshund.

"L ong, low, and tubular" epitomizes our spatial picture of the Dachshund. Obviously, the Dachshund would not have been nicknamed the "frankfurter dog" unless its gestalt were perceived as essentially long and tubular like a frankfurter. But is it not possible that the physical similarity of the Dachshund's body to a frankfurter has been unduly exaggerated in the popular mind by back formation with its "frankfurter" epithet as well as by other psychological effects? How truly does the mental cartoon of an ambulatory hot dog correspond to the actual quantitative proportions of the Dachshund's body?

Certainly, with its dandelion-scattering three-inch clearance, the Dachshund rates about as "low" as a dog can go. By the measure of its appendicular length ratio, L/H—where L is body-length (point-of-brisket to point-of-buttock) and H is body-height (top-of-withers to ground)—the Dachshund also qualifies as a "long" dog: for a Dachshund's $L/H \approx 2$ (versus a normal hound's $L/H \approx 1$). Yet, as measured by its axial length ratios—namely, body-length to body-width and body-length to head-length—the Dachshund does not qualify as abnormally long but falls comfortably within the normal range for hounds. Inspection of the transverse cross-section of the Dachshund's trunk, finally, reveals it to be not abnormally "tubular" but instead a quite normal Cassinian oval.

Conduct, if you will, the following thought experiment in switching the appendicular carriages of two dogs. First, cut the legs (including the scapulae and pelvic girdle) off a Standard Dachshund (D) and off some normal hound—say, a Deutsche Bracke (B)—that has the same-sized head. Next, attach the Bracke legs ($legs_B$)in the appropriate order to the Dachshund trunk ($trunk_D$)and vice versa. Now, compare the bodily proportions of your surgical hybrids to those of the presurgical breed specimens.

Hybrid $trunk_D + legs_B$ will be seen to exhibit all the proportions of a normal Bracke—not those of an abnormally long-bodied Bracke. Similarly, hybrid $trunk_B + legs_D$ will be seen to exhibit all the proportions of a normal Dachshund—not those of an abnormally short-bodied Dachshund. That the body of the Dachshund appears to us "long and tubular" like a frankfurter turns out to be a psychological self-deception.

When confronted by deviant proportions in a familiar cruciform object, our norm-craving brains seek to mitigate the actual shortening of one principal element by an illusory lengthening of the transverse principal element. Just as the body of a caterpillar seems less long to our senses if framed by outstretched butterfly wings, so the real

Dachondroplasia

truncation of the Dachshund's legs is parlayed into a perceptual elongation of the Dachshund's body. In quantitative as opposed to perceptual terms, the Dachshund somatype can much more fittingly be described as a composition of two discrete proportional domains: a

normally-proportioned hound's head and trunk decoupaged onto abnormally short legs.

The key element of the Dachshund's physical type, then, is simply the shortness of its limbs. The Dachshund's abnormally short limbs are the somatic expression of an underlying genetic abnormality. In this chapter, we will trace the roots of the Dachshund's body-form in the phenomenon of dwarfism and compare the Dachshund to other dwarf breeds. We will show that the conformation of the purebred Standard Dachshund depends on a particular dwarfing mutation in its genotype; and that the conformation of the Miniature Dachshund depends on the simultaneous operation of two separate dwarfing mutations. Especial comparative reference will be made to dwarfing mutations in Pugs (representative of the end-member dog breeds whose conformation depends on four separate dwarfing mutations) and in human beings.

The present chapter on genetics is unabashedly slanted to deep-digging Dachsomaniacs. Less gung-ho readers who find the helical thread of this chapter spooling underground to depths too gloomy for comfort are encouraged to back out and trot ahead to the sunny chapters on Dachshund history—where the truffles all lie much nearer the surface. But for those not disinclined to go to earth, we now hasten after the late *Beagle* naturalist as he dives down the hole of canine heredity.

Nowhere did Charles Darwin more explicitly develop his revolutionary idea that species evolve by an incessant interplay between variation and selection than with reference to the origin of dog breeds. In the first volume of his monumental *The Variation of Animals and Plants under Domestication* (1868), Darwin recognized in dog breeds two general classes of inherited traits, distinguished by their contrasting modes of variation and selection. Traits of the first type are those that have arisen through "the selection, both methodical and unconscious, of slight individual differences,—the latter kind of selection resulting from the occasional preservation, during hundreds of generations, of those individual dogs which were the most useful to man for certain purposes and under certain conditions of life."

In contrast to this first—what might now be termed *adaptive*—class of traits fixed by insensibly incremental selection of slight differences (nowadays called *allelomorphic variants*) according to largely unconscious criteria of usefulness for a complex of work functions, inherited traits of Darwin's second class are those that have arisen through the deliberate preservation of radical mutations. "A peculiarity suddenly arising, and therefore in one sense deserving to be called a monstrosity, may, however, be increased and fixed by man's selection." As two instances of this second class of inherited traits in dog breeds, Darwin cites "the shape of the legs and body in the turnspit of Europe and India; the shape of the head and the under-hanging jaw in the bull- and pug-dog, so alike in this one respect and so unlike in all others."

"Turnspit legs" and "pug-dog head": These two examples of Darwin's second, *non-adaptive* class of inherited traits in dog breeds are both manifestations of a genetic disorder called *achondroplasia*. Any genetic disorder in a dog breed that causes certain bones to grow to a length that is disproportionately short in relation to the rest of the skeleton falls under the rubric of *achondroplasia*. Achondroplasia (literally, "without cartilage formation") acts by inhibiting cartilage formation at certain of the discrete *epiphyseal growth plate* sites distributed throughout the skeleton. Depending on which particular epiphyseal growth plate sites are affected, various achondroplasias are seen to affect specific bones in the different achondroplastic dog breeds. "Turnspit legs" exemplify what is now termed *micromelic achondroplasia*; "pug-dog head" exemplifies *brachycephalic achondroplasia*.

Micromelic achondroplasia targets only the epiphyseal growth plate sites at the proximal ends of the long bones and thus acts to shorten only the dog's limbs, without appreciably affecting its axial skeleton (head, trunk, and tail). The Dachshund and Basset breeds—modern successors of the extinct Turnspit—exemplify the variety of achondroplasia that causes *micromelia* ("small limbs"). On account of their abnormally short stature, the micromelic breeds rank as *dwarves* in the general zoological sense. But since their axial skeletons generally retain normal size and proportion, the micromelic dog breeds are more narrowly classified zoologically as *achondroplastic* (or *disproportionate*) *dwarves*. (In the nomenclature of the dog fancy, it should be noted, the term *dwarf* is reserved exclusively for *proportionate* dwarves.)

Opposed to the disproportionate effects of achondroplastic dwarfism are the proportionate effects of *pituitary dwarfism*—as seen in dozens of toy breeds such as the Chihuahua, the Pomeranian, the Italian Greyhound, and the Miniature Pinscher. The small stature of the pituitary (or *ateliotic*) dwarf (non-technically, *midget*) results not from any site-specific achondroplastic disorder but rather from a systemic endocrine disturbance (deficient secretion of the hormone *somatrophin* by the anterior lobe of the pituitary gland) that acts to stunt all somatic cell growth proportionally. The stunted features often assume an infantile or neotenic character. Ateliosis is a genetic disorder transmitted as a recessive condition.

Clearly, not all dwarf breeds are achondroplastic. Yet the converse is also true: not all achondroplastic breeds are dwarves. Brachycephalic achondroplasia shortens just the face of a dog. Because leg-length is unaffected, facially achondroplastic breeds are—all other things being equal—not dwarves. The Boxer, the Dogue de Bordeaux, and the Bullmastiff represent the category of non-dwarf achondroplastics.

Given that brachycephalic achondroplasia, micromelic achondroplasia, and ateliosis all operate independently of each other but not necessarily exclusively of each other in a given individual dog, a scheme of eight possible combinations arises within which all dog breeds can be categorized:

1) brachycephalic achondroplastic/non-ateliotic (e.g., Boxer);

2) brachycephalic achondroplastic/ateliotic (e.g., Boston Terrier);

3) micromelic achondroplastic/non-ateliotic (e.g., Dachshund);

4) micromelic achondroplastic/ateliotic (e.g., Miniature Dachshund);

5) brachycephalic + micromelic achondroplastic/non-ateliotic (e.g., Bulldog);

6) brachycephalic + micromelic achondroplastic/ateliotic (e.g., Pug);

7) non-achondroplastic/non-ateliotic (e.g., German Shepherd Dog);

8) non-achondroplastic/ateliotic (e.g., Chihuahua).

As a further complication to the above scheme, two topologically distinct brachycephalic achondroplasias are inferred to operate in dogs. One form of brachycephalic achondroplasia specifically inhibits the chondrification of Meckel's cartilage in the first visceral arch and so shortens the lower jaw (the *mandible*). The other form of brachycephalic achondroplasia inhibits membranous ossification at the anterior and posterior basicranial epiphyseal growth plate sites and so shortens just the upper face and upper jaw (the *maxillary* region). When mandibular shortening is slight, maxillary achondroplasia results in the strongly undershot lower jaw (*mandibular prognathism*) that characterizes the modern English Bulldog, the Boxer, and the Dogue de Bordeaux.

Yet milder forms of mandibular prognathism occur chronically as undesirable aberrations in all dog

breeds with achondroplastic heads. The failure of many generations of breeders to eliminate recurrent structural disharmony between opposing jaws in these breeds—together with the highly heterogeneous jaw configurations recorded in the second filial generations of Charles Stockard's extensive hybridization experiments with achondroplastic dog breeds reported in *The Genetic and Endocrinic Basis for Differences in Form and Behavior* (1941)—demonstrate that mandibular achondroplasia and maxillary achondroplasia are essentially separate disorders, each under independent genetic determination. The implication is that the flat-faced dog breeds (such as the Brussels Griffon) in fact evince a *double achondroplasia*—both maxillary and mandibular achondroplasias at once.

The most completely achondroplastic dog breeds are the toy imports of East Asian origin that are classified in our Group 6 ("brachycephalic + micromelic achondroplastic/ateliotic dogs"): the Pekingese, the Shih Tzu, and the Pug. The body-forms of these *triply achondroplastic* breeds represent the simultaneous superposition of all three varieties of achondroplasia—micromelic, maxillary, and mandibular—on a midget frame. Thus, the Pug's disproportionately stumpy legs, tending to bow (*genu varum*), result from micromelic achondroplasia. The Pug's bulging forehead (*frontal bossing*); large, starting eyes (*exophthalmos*); pronounced stop (*recessed nasion*); and short midface (*midface hypoplasia*) all reflect maxillary achondroplasia. The Pug's short lower jaw expresses mandibular achondroplasia. The Pug's extraordinarily flat face and crowded dentition are accidents of the simultaneous operation of maxillary and mandibular achondroplasia.

Although achondroplastic dwarfism apparently occurs at characteristic frequencies in all higher animal species, it tends to be naturally selected only under extraordinary circumstances of biogeographical insularity. By contrast, achondroplastic dwarf races have been developed and perpetuated by artificial selection in virtually all species of domesticated animal: dog, cat, horse, cow, buffalo, pig, sheep, goat, rabbit, and chicken.

Achondroplasia—the most common variety of dwarfism in man—occurs in all human populations at a fairly constant frequency of about 1 in every 26,000 births. Human achondroplasia is readily diagnosed by a definite set of extreme somatic expressions that are remarkably similar in character to those of the dog breeds of Group 6. Like the Pug's, the limbs of the human achondroplastic dwarf are shortened by rhizomelic micromelia and tend to *genu varum*. Like the Pug's, the head of the human achondroplastic dwarf exhibits frontal bossing; exophthalmos; recessed nasion; midface hypoplasia; pug nose; respiratory stenosis; malocclusion; and crowded dentition.

Although human achondroplastic dwarves and Pugs show these surprisingly strong external (*phenotypic*) resemblances, they differ fundamentally in the manner in which their respective achondroplasias are genetically determined and transmitted (that is, in their *genotypes*). In the first place, human achondroplastic dwarves inherit both micromelia of the limbs and facial shortening as a unitary syndrome; whereas—as we have seen—Pugs inherit micromelia of the limbs, maxillary shortening, and mandibular shortening as separate and independent traits. In the second place, human achondroplasia is transmitted as a dominant condition with complete penetrance; whereas each of the three localized achondroplasias operative in the Pug breed is transmitted as a dominant condition with incomplete penetrance. In the third place, human achondroplastic dwarves display normal trunk dimensions; whereas Pugs display the miniature trunk dimensions of the ateliotic dwarf.

Let us enlarge our consideration of each of these three contrasts in achondroplastic style to dogs in general. We look first at the species contrast between achondroplasia as a singular syndrome in human beings and as a manifold of separable traits in dogs. In 1994, several research groups reported the unique cause of human achondroplasia to be a point mutation on the distal region of the short arm of chromosome 4, such that the arginine is substituted for glycine in a single nucleotide in the transmembrane domain of the gene called Fibroblast Growth Factor Receptor 3 (FGFR 3). This gene encodes the growth factor receptors that regulate cartilage growth plate differentiation. The arginine substitution (Arg 380) disrupts signal transduction through FGFR 3 so that bones develop dystrophically at the epiphyseal growth plate sites. According to the research groups, this single mis-scripted amino acid determines all the physical manifestations of achondroplasia in human beings.

Even though the chromosomal loci for achondroplasia in dogs have yet to be pinpointed, we may predict that the biochemical etiology of canine achondroplasia will not prove as simple as reported in the human case. Biochemists working in the Dog Genome project at Berkeley regard as plausible the hypothesis that an analogous point mutation in FGFR3 will eventually be found to determine achondroplasia in dogs. But recall the several, highly localized achondroplastic effects that we see variously combined in the gamut of achondroplastic dog breeds: the Standard Dachshund with its achondroplastic legs but normal head; the Boxer with its achondroplastic upper jaw but normal legs; the Boston Terrier with its achondroplastic upper jaw, achondroplastic lower jaw, but normal legs; the English Bulldog with its achondroplastic upper jaw and achondroplastic legs; and, most extensively, the Pug with its achondroplastic upper jaw, achondroplastic lower jaw,

and achondroplastic legs.

Separability of traits in expression implies independence of transmission. The Pug's achondroplasia must be the result of at least three separate genetic defects. In respect of dwarfing as of so many other physical characteristics, the 78 chromosomes of *Canis familiaris* would appear to harbor a richer diversity of potential somatic expression than the 46 chromosomes of *Homo sapiens*.

An alternative interpretation, however, is suggested by the occurrence in human populations of a rarer disproportionate dwarfism called pseudoachondroplasia. The *pseudoachondoplastic* dwarf has micromelic limbs but a normal face and skull. The separability of micromelia in expression allows that the Arg 380 point mutation reported in 1994 might be a necessary but not sufficient cause of human achondroplasia. In other words, the reported mutation might determine either micromelic achondroplasia or facial achondroplasia rather than both as a unitary syndrome. If some other point mutation is eventually found to be epistatically linked to the Arg 380 mutation as a cofactor in human achondroplasia, then the chromosomal templates for human and canine achondroplasias—in particular, for human pseudoachondroplasia and freestanding canine micromelic achondroplasia as exemplified in the Dachshund—might prove in the future to be somewhat more analogous than they now appear.

We turn to the second contrast between human and canine achondroplastics: Just as the genetic controls on achondroplasia are less simple in dogs than in human beings, so the modes of inheritance are more complex in dogs. Human achondroplasia is transmitted as a *dominant condition with complete penetrance. Dominance* here means that if an individual carries the Arg 380-mutation in his genotype, he will be an achondroplastic dwarf in his phenotype. *Complete*

penetrance means that the phenotype of an individual who is heterozygous for the Arg 380-mutation (that is, one of whose two homologous FGFR3-genes is mutated by arginine-substitution) will be as symptomatically achondroplastic as that of a homozygous individual (that is, both of whose FGFR3-genes are so mutated). In terms of heritability, these conditions translate into simple probabilities: if both human parents are heterozygous achondroplastic dwarves, then—on average—75% of their progeny will be achondroplastic dwarves and 25% will be normal in phenotype.

By contrast, none of the three achondroplasias found in dogs is transmitted as a dominant condition with complete penetrance. Micromelic achondroplasia in dogs is transmitted as a dominant condition with *incomplete penetrance*; meaning that a dog whose genotype is heterozygous for the micromelic mutation will have distinctly longer legs than its homozygous dwarf sibling.

In terms of heritability, if both dog parents are heterozygous for the micromelic mutation in their genotypes, then—on average—25% of their progeny will be micromelic achondroplastic dwarves in phenotype; 50% will

show intermediate leg-length; and 25% will show normal leg-length. If one dog parent is heterozygous but the other is homozygous for the micromelic mutation, then—on average—50% of their progeny will be micromelic achondroplastic dwarves in phenotype and 50% will show intermediate leg-length. If both dog parents are homozygous for the micromelic mutation in their genotypes, then necessarily 100% of their progeny will be micromelic achondroplastic dwarves in phenotype.

Clearly, if an individual progenitor is heterozygous with respect to the micromelic mutation, its progeny will be statistically mixed in phenotype. But the Dachshund is a breed: Dachshunds bred to Dachshunds always throw Dachshunds. Since 100% of Dachshund-to-Dachshund progeny are achondroplastic in phenotype, we must infer that all Dachshunds are homozygotes with

respect to micromelic achondroplasia.

The third and final contrast between human and canine achondroplasias that we consider is that only the latter may be overprinted by ateliosis. Standard Dachshunds, for example, are dwarfed in stature by micromelic achondroplasia; apart from their limbs, they are normal in size. Notwithstanding their achondroplastic dwarfism, Standard Dachshund populations also throw ateliotic dwarves at a low but definite frequency. In the past century, ateliotic Dachshunds have been deliberately preserved and interbred in order to establish a distinct sub-breed for show—the Miniature Dachshund.

Every Miniature Dachshund is thereby doubly dwarfed, being at once an achondroplastic and an ateliotic dwarf. We have already noted that canine achondroplasias are transmitted as dominant conditions with incomplete penetrance; and that canine ateliosis is transmitted as a recessive condition. Consequently, if an individual were heterozygous with respect to either condition, its progeny would necessarily be mixed in phenotype. But the Miniature Dachshund is an established breed, such that Miniature Dachshunds bred to Miniature Dachshunds always throw Miniature Dachshunds. Since 100% of Miniature Dachshund progeny are both achondroplastic and ateliotic in phenotype, all Miniature Dachshunds are homozygotes with respect to both achondroplasia and ateliosis.

We rest our demonstration of what we set out at the beginning of this chapter to show: that the conformation of the purebred Standard Dachshund depends on one particular dwarfing mutation in its genotype; and that the conformation of the Miniature Dachshund depends on the simultaneous operation of two separate dwarfing mutations. Having dispatched our deep-secreted quarry, let us joyfully return to the surface to root for dessert in the loose dirt of Dachshund history.

The Dachshund is a basset. Before the Dachshund fancy sets off in full cry after the author of such an impudent assertion, allow him to hedge his statement. Ahem...linguistically and morphologically, the Dachshund has for most of its history been indistinguishable from the basset.

Linguistically—from its first attested appearance in the German language at the end of the seventeenth century until well into the nineteenth century—the word *Dachshund* explicitly and exactly translated the older French word *basset*. *Dachshund* first appears in 1682 in a work by the Austrian writer von Hohberg (*Georgica*, cited below), who treats of badger hunting in a passage openly borrowed from a much older classic French work by Du Fouilloux dating to 1560 (*La Vénerie*, see below). Von Hohberg employs the word *Dachshund* as his translation into German of the French word in Du Fouilloux: *Basset*. In turn, von Hohberg's text served as the model for German writing on badger hunting for the next century (see below: von Fleming, 1719; Döbel, 1746)—so that the French word *Basset* underlies the word *Dachshund* in German texts of the eighteenth century, too.

For almost two centuries after von Hohberg's first use of the German word, *Dachshund* and *Basset* continued to convey an identical sense, compounded equally of a functional and of a physical element. Functionally, both

words—*Dachshund* and *Basset*—signified a dog that was employed by the hunter to go to earth after fossorial vermin—especially badger and fox (see Nicot 1606, below). This functional identity of the *Dachshund* and *basset* as badger-dogs endured until the nineteenth century.

Only in the second half of the nineteenth century did the diffusion of the breech-loading rabbit rifle transform the primary function of the French basset into that of an aboveground trailer in the *chasse au tir* of hares and rabbits. In the eighteenth century, bassets were occasionally put to use as trailers in hare-shooting as an employment secondary to their earth-going function (see Döbel 1746, below). Much more commonly, however, the traditional relays of harriers were used to run down lagomorph quarry either to exhaustion or else to ground (where the plodding bassets then took over the end game). Only in response to nineteenth-century improvements to sporting pieces did the primary job of the basset change from earth-dog to slow-speed scent-trailer.

The basset's superb nose enabled it to pick up and follow a lagomorph's trail. The basset's shortness of

The Low-down on Dachshunds and Bassets

leg afforded the dual advantage of allowing the shooter to keep up with his dog and of lulling the lagomorph quarry into desultory stop-and-go flight, so that the shooter might get off a close-range shot with his newly accurate small-bore weapon without endangering his slow-moving trailing dogs. The basset's changed sporting function contributed to widening divergences in conformation between the evolving Basset breeds and the comparatively conservative Dachshund breeds in the second half of the nineteenth century. It was during this period that the French hunting literature first distinguished the Dachshund as a recognized basset subtype—namely, the *basset allemand* (Gayot *Le Chien*, 1867). The French basset breeds were tending to become larger in size, heavier in build, and more pendulously bloodhoundish in the muzzle.

In late nineteenth-century Germany, by contrast, dachshund breeds were tending to become smaller. Sporting dachshunds continued to be regarded as earth-dogs first and foremost and so were kept large enough to fight underground. But non-working dachshund strains were yielding to aesthetic pressure to shrink in size. One of the aesthetic desiderata promoted by the new Dachshund breeding clubs that started up in Germany at the close of the nineteenth century was refinement of facial structure, a quality that tends to be conjoined to smaller body size. In the twentieth century, smallness in Dachshunds became elevated to an aesthetic ideal unto itself with the establishment of the Miniature Dachshund breeds.

Nonetheless, down through the three centuries preceding the divergence of the breeds—from the mid-sixteenth through the mid-nineteenth centuries—the words *Dachshund* and *basset* had referred to dogs that did the same kind of work and looked essentially alike. The physical element of the meanings of both terms signified a dog that was extremely short-legged but otherwise normally-proportioned. Recall the conclusion of our surgical thought experiment in Chapter

2: "The Dachshund somatype can much more fittingly be described as a composition of two discrete proportional domains: a normally-proportioned hound's head and trunk decoupaged onto abnormally short legs." Exactly the same conclusion—but about French Bassets—was enunciated by their foremost breeder and exponent in the nineteenth century, le comte le Couteulx de Canteleu (*Manuel de Vénerie Française*, 1890): "The general form of the Bassets [is] hounds (*chiens courants*) with a body and head identical to the big dogs, but with such short legs—whether crooked or straight (*torses ou droites*)—that the body has the air of being supported by the ground."

Comte le Couteulx divided Bassets into two subtypes based on leg conformation: crooked or straight. (The Count's own strain of smooth tricolor Basset was straight-legged; M. Lane's strain of the white and lemon-colored Basset was crooked-legged. Between them, comte le Couteulx and M. Lane claimed to have resurrected the original *Basset à l'Artois et à la Flandre* as described by Du Fouilloux in 1560. The modern *Basset Artésien Normand* was developed at the close of the nineteenth century by a blending of these two private lines.) It is no accident that, from the sixteenth century onwards, authorities in both France (see below, e.g.: Du Fouilloux, 1560; Daubenton, 1758) and Germany (see below, e.g.: von Hohberg, 1682; von Hoppe, 1761) consistently divided their respective *bassets* and *Dachshunds* into the very same physical subtypes: crooked-legged as opposed to straight-legged; and rough-haired as opposed smooth. As depicted in eighteenth-century book illustrations in France (see below: Daubenton, 1758) and Germany (see below: Riedel, 1780), the *Dachshund* subtypes are indistinguishable from the corresponding *basset* subtypes .

Even today, eighteenth-century drawings of *Bassets* are routinely passed off as drawings of *Dachshunds*. It is a time-honored practice in English-language books on the Dachshund breed to reproduce the two-figure plate from Daubenton (1758) that illustrates his chapter on Bassets. To their reproductions of this plate, Dachshund authors (Sanborn, 1937; Meistrell, 1976; Adler, 1977; Hutchinson & Hutchinson, 1997) invariably put the caption: "Crooked and straight-legged **Dachshunds**, according to Buffon." None of these authors bothers to mention that the original French captioning reads: *"Le Basset à jambes torses"* and *"Le Basset à jambes droites"*; or that the word *Dachshund* appears nowhere in the original French work (composed of two parts, written by Buffon and his colleague Daubenton, respectively)!

So late as 1880, a dog expert could still argue that there was no real morphological distinction between certain Bassets and Dachshunds. In *British Dogs: Their Varieties, History, Characteristics, Breeding, Management* and *Exhibition*, published in London in 1879-80, Hugh Dalziel quotes a contemporary British breeder writing under the pen-name, *Wildfowler*: "A black and tan or red *Basset à jambes torses* cannot by any possible use of one's eyes be distinguished from a Dachshund of the same colour, although some German writers assert that the breeds are quite distinct."

Today, six Basset breeds are recognized by the FCI: the Basset Artésien Normand; the Basset Bleu de Gascogne; the Grand Basset Griffon Vendéen; the Petit Basset Griffon Vendéen; the Basset Fauve de Bretagne; and the Basset Hound. The last-named Basset breed—the familiar one whose narrow head, pendulous flews, baggy skin, huge pendent ears, and lugubrious eyes have been found strangely effective in persuading Americans to buy shoes—is English, having been developed between 1866 and 1875 in three English kennels that cooperatively crossed several private strains of imported Norman basset stock. The other five Basset breeds are strictly homegrown French. Of these, the first two (the Basset Artésien

Normand and the Basset Bleu de Gascogne) are smooth-coated; the other three are rough-coated.

Of the five current French basset breeds, the smooth, tricolored Basset Artésien Normand has inherited the highest proportion of the broader-headed, smaller-eared, tighter-skinned, crooked-legged nineteenth-century breed called Basset Artois, which was reputed to have descended from the old Artésien basset stock that Du Fouilloux recommended to his readers way back in 1560 as the best for badger hunting: "There are different varieties of bassets. One variety of bassets, which we believe came out of the Artois region of Flanders, have crooked legs and are generally short-haired. Another variety of bassets are rough-haired and straight-legged. The variety of bassets with crooked legs will take the earth better than the other, and are better for badger hunting, because they are better able to press their prey by staying underground longer." These crooked-legged, short-haired bassets from Artois are figured in the two woodcuts illustrating Du Fouilloux' text on badger hunting (see below).

The other smooth-haired modern French basset breed—the Basset Bleu de Gascogne—bears a remarkable resemblance to the *Basset à jambes torses* figured in Daubenton (1758). Every detail in this eighteenth-century image corresponds to a standard point of the modern Basset Bleu: legs dwarfed but not extremely so; wrists bent outward but not knuckled over; forehead broad but nose pointed; ears pendent but not immoderately large; skin loose but not baggy; smooth coat tricolored but predominantly white roaned toward "blue".

We now have the premises for a provocative syllogism. First Premise: The modern French Basset Bleu looks just like the *Basset à jambes* torses figured in Daubenton (1758). Second Premise: Daubenton's figure of the Basset *à jambes torses* is unanimously labeled *"Dachshund"* by modern authors of books about Dachshunds. Conclusion: Therefore any modern expert

on the Dachshund will not scruple to label the modern French Basset Bleu a Dachshund.

Of course, any Dachshund expert would sooner lop off his or her hand than suffer it to write *"Dachshund"* below a photograph of a Basset Bleu. But the silliness of our syllogistic conclusion reveals a subtler absurdity at work in the real world of the dog fancy. We submit that the minor morphological difference between the Basset Bleu and the Dachshund has been perceptually exaggerated by nomenclatural difference and national stereotyping. On an ingenuous palate, will not the same wine conjure up quite different associative ecstasies depending whether the label pasted on the bottle reads "Château d'Yquem" or "Schloss Johannisberg"? *Wildfowler* (*ibid.*) makes essentially the same point about a Norman variety of *Bassets à jambes torses* (precursors of the modern Basset Artésien Normand) and Dachshunds of the late nineteenth century: "To the naked eye there is no difference, but in the matter of names (wherein German scientists particularly shine) then, indeed, confusion gets worse confounded."

To our ears a century later, Wildfowler's claim sounds way overstated (not to mention chauvinistic). Today there are obvious differences between the Standard Smooth Dachshund and the smooth French Basset breeds. Both the Basset Artésien Normand and the Basset Bleu differ from the Standard Smooth Dachshund not only in coat color but also in being about one-third heavier in weight and longer of leg. In overall conformation, nevertheless, it cannot be denied that the two smooth French Basset breeds and the Standard Smooth Dachshund still look strikingly alike.

In *Hounds of the World* (1937), no less astute a judge of braccoidal flesh than Sir John Buchanan-Jardine opines: "Gascogne Bassets remind one very strongly of German Dachshunds: the general build is very similar, which, with the pointed nose, helps increase the resemblance." Indeed, any unprejudiced observer will admit that the Basset Bleu resembles the Standard Smooth Dachshund in overall conformation more closely than it does any of the other modern Basset breeds except perhaps for the Basset Artésien Normand. By this standard of comparison, the Dachshund is more of a basset than most Bassets are!

Confirming these qualitative judgments, hard quantitative evidence for the morphological congruence between the historical French smooth Basset breeds and the modern Dachshund is furnished in Daubenton (1758). As shown in the table below, Daubenton's measurements of ten diagnostic length parameters in the *Basset à jambes torses* prove to be all but identical to those of a modern Dachshund scaled to the same overall body length.

The long and the short of it: the Dachshund is a basset. The fine print: this is a statement of formal identity based on synonymous historical usage and on morphological similarities. Disclaimer: this is not a genetic statement. It does not say that Dachshunds "came from" bassets.

It may or may not be true that modern German Dachshunds are descended from old French bassets—or *vice versa*, for that matter. The historical evidence is far too meager to settle the biological question of whether modern Bassets and Dachshunds developed from a common ancestor or else independently. One line of modern physical evidence, however, tends to favor the latter explanation—namely, that French Bassets and German Dachshunds developed in parallel independence.

The pertinent observation is that each of the modern French Basset breeds is formally paired with its own modern normally-proportioned hound breed: the Basset Artésien Normand has as its normal counterpart the Chien d'Artois; the Basset Bleu de Gascogne has its Grand

Bleu de Gascogne; the Grand Basset Griffon Vendéen has its Grand Griffon Vendéen; the Petit Basset Griffon Vendéen has its Briquet Griffon Vendéen; and the Basset Fauve de Bretagne has its Griffon Fauve de Bretagne. Likewise, each one of the modern FCI-recognized Swiss Niederlaufhund (short-legged scenthound) breeds is formally paired with its own modern normally-proportioned scenthound breed: the Schweizer Niederlaufhund has as its normal counterpart the Schweizer Laufhund; the Jura Niederlaufhund has its Bruno Jura Laufhund; the Berner Niederlaufhund has its Berner Laufhund; and the Luzerner Niederlaufhund has its Luzerner Laufhund.

The strong implication is that each modern French Basset or Swiss Niederlaufhund breed was developed independently of all other Basset or Niederlaufhund breeds by artificial selection for the micromelic achondroplasia mutation within the same circumscribed normal-sized hound breeding population from which the modern normal-sized counterpart breed is descended. By this view, for example, the Basset Bleu de Gascogne was developed by breeders selecting for dwarfing mutations in the ancestors of the Grand Bleu de Gascogne, such that the Basset Bleu de Gascogne shares no common dwarf ancestor with, say, the Basset Fauve de Bretagne.

Analogy suggests that the Dachshund was developed by a similar process of internal selection within a pre-existent Austro-German hound breed—in all probability, some proto-Bracke or -Schweisshund breed. The modern FCI-recognized Austro-German Bracke breeds include the Deutsche Bracke (the successor breed to the historic Westfalische Bracke, Sauerlander Holzbracke, and Steinbracke breeds); the Westfalische Dachsbracke; the Alpenlandischer Dachsbracke; the Tyroler Bracke; the Steirischer Rauhaarige Hochgebirgsbracke; and the Osterreichischer Glatthaariger Bracke. The modern FCI-recognized Austro-German

Schweisshund breeds include the Bayrischer Gebirgs-schweisshund and the Hannoverscher Schweisshund.

Superficially, the modern Austro-German non-Dachshund hound breed that looks in the face most like the late-eighteenth to early-nineteenth-century Dachshunds is the short- (but not dwarf-) legged Alpenlandischer Dachsbracke. The modern Austro-German non-Dachshund hound breed that looks in the face most like the late-nineteenth and modern Dachshunds is the normal-legged Bayrischer Gebirgsschweisshund. Interestingly, both these scenthound breeds were developed in mountainous regions. Fitzinger (1867, cited below) states his belief that the Dachshund/Basset archetype "originated in the higher mountain ranges of of Southern and Middle Europe, in particular the Pyrenees and Alps." Such an origin would be consonant with the relatively high frequency of genetic abnormalities in small inbred populations. In the closed populations of isolated alpine valleys, spontaneous mutations such as micromelic achondroplasia would certainly stand a better chance of being inherited.

If our hunch about the multiple derivations of the dwarf-legged breeds is correct, the disproportionately high number of dwarf-legged breeds that have been spun off from the normally-proportioned hound breeds might reflect greater scope for breeder selection resulting from a higher frequency of spontaneous micromelic achondroplasia mutation in the Hound Family (*Braccoides*) than in other dog breed families such as the Greyhound Family (*Graioides*) and the Wolf Family (*Lupoides*). By implication, future breeders could theoretically exploit spontaneous mutations to re-develop any one of the existing dwarf-legged breeds from scratch, starting only with the normal-sized counterpart breed.

Such a stark picture of completely independent evolution for each variety of achondroplastically short-legged hound (or *basset*, in the wider sense that includes dachshunds) is doubtless overdrawn. The hybrid origin of the English Basset, for one, is a matter of record. Importations and interminglings amongst basset lineages probably modified the ancestral stock of all the modern basset breeds to some extent. Nevertheless, the pattern of normal/dwarf counterpart breeds described above does support the predominance of the process of independent evolution over that of radiative dispersion in the development of the basset breeds. The broad morphological simi-

larity that we have noted among the Basset Bleu de Gascogne, the Basset Artésien Normand, and the Standard Smooth Dachshund probably owes much more to the broad morphological similarity among their parent breeds—the ancestors of the Grand Bleu de Gascogne, the Chien d'Artois, and the Deutsche Bracke, respectively— than it does to radial descent of all three breeds from some hypothetical dwarf-legged common ancestor.

So much for handwaving and tailwagging. Now for chapter and verse. To allow the reader to judge how well our interpretive account of the early history of dachshunds squares with the historical record, we cite (in order of year of first publication) all documentary references containing the word *Dachshund* (which will be editorially emboldened where it or its synonyms occur in the body of any citation) that we could find from the period extending from the first printed occurrence of the word *Dachshund* in 1682 until the end of the eighteenth century. Editorial interpolations within a citation (whether editorial glosses or italicized key expressions as rendered in the original language) are enclosed by brackets and printed in a contrasting font. Most citations are prefaced by an editorial remark about the author and his sources. All translations in this and the next chapter are the present author's, except where explicitly noted otherwise.

The extensive 16th-18th-century citations are followed by summary mention of some early 19th-century descriptions of Dachshund varieties as gleaned from Herbert S. Sanborn's classic monograph, *The Dachshund or Teckel* (1937). Our review of the early Dachshund literature concludes with an extended excerpt on Dachshund types from a taxonomy of dog breeds published in 1867 by a German biologist with a textbook case of Linnaean dementia. It provides us a formal portrait of the extraordinarily diverse Dachshund Group as it was viewed in Germany just prior to the dawn of the Dachshund breeding clubs.

•1682   Wolfgang **von Hohberg**: *Georgica Curiosa Aucta.*

The earliest attested occurrence of the word *Dachshund* appears in the third volume of an extraordinary work of the Austrian Baroque era originally published in 1682: *Georgica Curiosa Aucta oder Adlichen Land- und Feld-Lebens auf alle in Deutschland übliche Land- und Haus-Wirtschafften* ("Comprehensive Agricultural Inquiries or Farming and Housekeeping proper to Aristocratic Country and Agrarian Life as practiced throughout Germany "), published in 3 volumes, written in German by the Austrian nobleman Wolfgang Helmhard **von Hohberg** (1612-1688) After serving as a Protestant officer in the Holy Roman Emperor's forces during the final Franco-Habsburg phase (1635-1648) of the Thirty Years War, Freiherr von Hohberg retired to the Bishopric of Regensburg (in modern Bavaria) in 1664, where he managed his own estates and wrote poetry. *Georgica* is a manual for the baroque gentleman living on his own estate, encompassing the whole spectrum of country life from child-delivery and horse-breeding to home-brewing and home-pharmacy (but, curiously enough, omitting any consideration of the management of inquisitive monkeys).

A full translation of Chapter 44 of Book 12, Vol. 3 of von Hohberg (ibid.) follows:

Of the **Badger**-, Otter- and Beaver-**Dogs**
[Von den Dachsen-, Otter- and Biber-Hunden]

These three sorts of dog-types [*Hunds-Gattungen*] are almost of identical function [*Verrichtung*]—that they must go to ground [*schlieffen*]—but the first [viz., *"die Dachsenhunde"* of the title] after badgers most of all; the latter having long, deep, sinuous burrows with usually more than one entrance. The dogs that are kept for that purpose [of going to badger earth] are called **Bassets** by the French, on account of their low stature; they have a long slender trunk [*langen schmalen Leib*] and low little feet [*niedrige Fusslein*], somewhat crooked [*eingeboge*], in order that they might all the better make progress in the burrow [*im Schlieffen*], for which reason they are also commonly called Burrower [*Schlieffer*] and Little Earth Dog [*Schlieff-Hündlein*]; they are all kinds

of colors, but mostly brown, gray, and brownish-gray [*braun, grau und Otterfarb*]—occasionally also black. [*n.b. Sanborn's (1937) paraphrase of this passage omits any reference to Bassets.*]

Mr. de Fouilloux distinguishes two breeds [*Arten*] of them [*Bassets*]: some smooth and crooked-legged [*glatt und krummfüssig*] and with shorter hair [*kurzer Haar*]; the others have straight legs [*gerade Schenckel*], and are snarl-haired [*stockhärig*] like the Water-Dogs. The former [breed: viz., the crooked-legged smooth Bassets] go eagerly to ground and are better for the badgers, as they stick it out underground longer and more patiently. The latter [breed: the straight-legged wirehaired Bassets] both run better on the ground and also attack more strongly in the burrow; yet since they exhaust themselves with their excessive fierceness, they must all the sooner come out to recover their breath. When they reach more than three-quarters of a year old, they are taken out side by side with old dogs but are kept on the outside, and the old badger-finders [*Dachsfinder*] alone are entered into the burrow, and the young are held in check at the entrance of the holes so that they might hear how the old ones bark and worry the badger with their teeth; thereafter when the badger is caught and half-dead, the young dogs may be set on it; or one can break off the canine teeth of the living badger and then set the young dogs on it side by side with the older; so that it cannot injure them too severely, in consideration that if they are bitten too much the first time, they lose heart and no longer have confidence to tackle such an animal with authority, and they also become reluctant to go to earth.

Du Fouilloux gives the advice that one should, at the time when the badgers have their young, train the young dogs such that, if one knows their burrow, one should first engage the old badger dogs [*Dachshunde*] and—once the old [badgers] are caught or driven out by the dogs, and only the young [badgers] are still inside—one should encourage the young dogs to enter the earth and thereupon attack and kill the young [badgers] within.

There are also big, strong badger dogs [*grosse starcke Dachshunde*] with which one goes out, along with a pair of little bloodhounds [*Spührhündlein*], at night in the fall when there is much fruit; and—since the badger is accustomed to forage at night outside his burrow under the fruit trees—they are sometimes trailed by the little bloodhounds and afterwards caught by the big dogs [*grosse starcke Dachshunde*]. The people must be furnished with two-pronged forks with which they might pin and preserve the badger, for otherwise the dogs might mangle it badly.

For otter and beaver, strong biting flushing hounds [*starcke bißige Stöber*] and scenthounds [*Spührhunde*] are required, which ought to have been trained to it from youth: but since information on these animals already appears in the foregoing Eleventh Book, in the interests of brevity, we would refer the kind reader thereto.

A partial translation of Chapter 79 of Book 12, Vol. 3 of von Hohberg (*ibid.*) follows:

How to Hunt Badgers
[Wie die Dachsen zu jagen]

How to train badger dogs and burrowers [*Dachsenhunde und Schlieffer*] has already been considered above and need not be repeated here. There are only two ways to catch badgers: either at night, where one knows a badger earth to be near, to watch with dogs at the windfall fruit and so to hunt them, for which good biting dogs and strong large hounds [*starcke Rüden*] are required, that once

the prey is seized are set on no more; and people with forks and staves be at hand, in order to stop the badger and prevent its flight. The other [way to catch badgers] is by day, whereby one can track down their earth with badger dogs [*Dachsen-hunde*], drive these same [badgers] out of their dens and catch them with forks and nooses; or else one must dig them out, for which purpose one brings digging tools. One should affix to the badger dogs [*Dachshunde*] collars with bells, so that the badger might defend itself the sooner and so injure them [the *Dachshunde*] the less— for the badger offers as much resistance against dogs as a wild pig—inasmuch as it [the badger] will be content to bark and defend itself on all sides. If one sees, however, that the dogs become exhausted and the bells full of dirt, one can again remove the collars from them...

[Prince Rupert, hunting near Lintz, Germany] with his digging-dog [*Budelhund*] that he had for the first time obtained out of England, came across a badger in a burrow and the dog went to earth after it. It happened that the dog, which was rather tall and of a larger kind, got stuck in the tunnel...It happened that the Prince, out of love for the dog, himself crawled so deep into the tunnel that he could reach the dog's hind feet and grab hold of them. When he no longer had the ability to crawl back out again on account of the narrowness of the place, and then his protruding feet began to wriggle madly, his people became aware of the emergency that he was stuck down there and began to pull him out strongly by the feet. So it happened that from ever deeper in the tunnel, first the Prince; then by his hands the dog; and then by the dog's teeth the badger, in a train together—or rather one after the other—were brought out.

The classic French work that von Hohberg acknowledges as the source of his information about badger dogs is *La Vénerie* (Poitiers, 1560) by Jacques **du Fouilloux** (1521-80), seigneur of an estate in Poitou. In his excerpts from Du Fouilloux, as we have seen, von Hohberg explicitly renders *bassets* in the original as *Dachshunde* in his translation. Also of relevance to our present concerns are certain of the crude woodcuts that illustrate *La Vénerie*.

Three of the woodcut illustrations in the original edition of *La Vénerie* depict the *bassets* of the text. The first woodcut shows the procession of a hunting expedition to a badger ground: a horse-drawn hunting cart bearing the seigneur (none other than Jacques du Fouilloux himself) and his teenaged consort trundles along, accompanied on foot by a pack of bassets and a corvée of serfs armed with digging tools. The raves of the open charrette are hung with wine-flasks. Equal parts St. Hubert and Humbert Humbert, the seigneurial author of *La Vénerie* gives himself up to venery in the lap of his Lolita while on his way to enter his hounds of venery down the badger holes.

The second woodcut depicts the seigneur engaged in this latter form of venery. He is passionately urging five of his young *bassets* to go to ground and engage the badgers, crying to them, "Crawl down to him, basset! Crawl down to him! Hoa! Sic 'em! Sic 'em!" ("*Coule a luy Basset, Coule a luy, hou, prenez prenez.*"). Richard Surflet translates this passage from Du Fouilloux as part of his *Maison rustique, or the countrie farmer* (London, 1600) [the first English translation of Charles Jean Liébault's *L'Agriculture et Maison Rustique* (Paris, 1564); itself primarily a translation of Charles Estienne's *Praedium rusticum* (Paris, 1554) but augmented by extensive supplementary assages lifted verbatim from Du Fouilloux (Poitiers,1560)]:

Couple up all the old earth dogs, and after let loose the young ones, incouraging them to take the earth, and crying unto them, "Creepe into them **basset**, creep into them."

The third woodcut depicts the seigneur directing his vassals as they dig into the underground fracas with an assortment of specialized digging implements. Impatiently awaiting the exhumation of the badger are a *basset* and a nobleman brandishing a huge pair of pincers.

Despite the crudity of their rendering, one can clearly see that the *bassets* in these three woodcuts are all extremely short-legged; that the front feet of some are crooked outwards; that their trunks are long and not tucked up; that their ears are pendent; that their muzzles are rather short; and their tails are held gaily concave-upwards and moderately feathered. The *bassets* pictured in *La Vénerie* resemble both the modern Basset and the modern Dachshund with respect to the legs, feet, trunk, and ears; they differ with respect to the muzzle and tail.

Du Fouilloux' *La Vénerie* enjoyed such perennial popularity throughout Europe that it went into a least twenty-four French editions and was translated in English (1575), German (1590), and Italian (1621). In his unattributed translation of *La Vénerie* into English, re-titled *The Noble Art of Venerie or Hunting* (1575), the Elizabethan diplomat and poet, George **Turberville** (1540-1610), does not—like Surflet (1600)—retain the word *basset*; rather, he everywhere translates *basset* as *terrier* (in the sense of "earth dog").

Although all but five of the fifty-four woodcuts illustrating Turberville's book were taken from Du Fouilloux' parent work, the three badger-hunting woodcuts just described were omitted. One might suspect that the reason for this omission is that the Elizabethan earth-dogs already resembled the modern rough-haired, prick-eared British terriers rather than the short-haired, pendent-eared bassets of Du Fouilloux. Against this hypothesis may be ranged three bits of contemporary evidence that French bassets were indeed familiar in Elizabethan England: in 1570, the implicit description of the British Terrier by Johannes Caius (cited below, Chapter 4) as a pendent-eared and baggy-lipped scenthound; in 1594, a speech from *A Midsummer Night's Dream* (cited below, Chapter 4) in which Shakespeare describes in copious detail what can only be a crooked-legged Basset (Du Fouilloux' *basset à jambes torses*); and, finally, in 1600, the direct translation by Surflet (cited above) of French *basset* into English "basset".

Excerpts from Turberville's translation (*ibid.*) of Du Fouilloux' *La Vénerie* that concern the earth-dogs used in badger hunting follow [*n.b.* the present author has

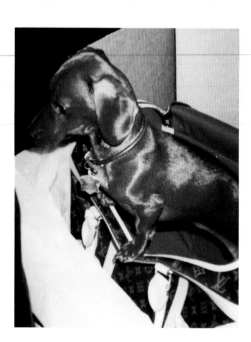

inserted certain words and phrases (in brackets) from Du Fouilloux' original French text immediately after the corresponding words or phrases (emboldened) of Turberville's translation]:

Chapter 65. Of the hunting of the Foxe and Badgerd.
[Chapitre 60. *Comme il faut dresser les petits Chiens de terre, pour la chasse des Regnardz et Tessons.*]

Now to speake of the **Foxhoundes and Terryers** [*Chiens de terre*] and how you should enter them to take the Foxe, the Badgerd, and such like vermine: you muste understand that there are sundrie sortes of **Terriers** [*Bassetz*], whereof we hold opinion that **one sorte came out of Flanders or the Lowe Countries, as Artoys and thereabouts** [*la race estre venüe des pays de Flandre, et d'Artoys*] and they have **crooked legges** [*les iambes torses*], and are short heared most commonly. Another sorte there is which are **shagged** [*à gros poil, comme Barbets*] and **streight legged** [*ont les iambes droites*]: those with crooked legges will **take the earth** [*coulent*] better than the other, and are better for the Badgerd, bycause they will lie longer at a vermine: but the others with streight legges do serve for two purposes, for they will Hunte above the ground aswell as the other hounds, and enter the earthe with more furie than the others: but they will not abide so long, bycause they are too eagre in fight, and therefore are con-streyned to come out and take the ayre: they are both good and badde of bothe sortes.

[Although Turberville's translation of Du Fouilloux is generally pretty good, he commits several serious errors of translation in the above passage that will be taken up in Ch. 4 of the present work. The corresponding text in Du Fouilloux' original follows:

*Apres auoir parlé de la chasse des Chiens courants, ie feray icy un petit traicté de la chasse des **Chiens de terre**, et comme on les doyt dresser pour prendre Regnardz, Tessons, & leurs semblables. Il faut entendre premièrement, que nous avons de deux espece de **Bassetz**, desquelz nous disons la race estre venüe des pays de Flandre, et d'Artoys: dont les vns ont les iambes torses, et sont communément à court poil: les autres ont les iambes droites, et sont volontiers à gros poil, comme Barbets. Ceux qui les ont torses, coulent plus aisément en la terre que les autres, et sont meilleurs pour les Blereaux,*

d'autant qu'ils y demeurent plus longuement, tenans mieux sans sortir. Ceux qui ont les iambes droictes, seruent à deux mestiers, par ce qu'ils courrent sur terre comme Chiens courans, et entreny de plus grand fureur et hardiesse en terre que les autres, mais ils n'y demeurent pas si longuement, d'autant qu'ils se tourmentent à combattre les Regnardz et Tessons, ce qui les contraint d'en sortir pour prendre air. Il s'en trouuent de bons et de mauuais des deux especes.

In *Thresor de la Langue Françoyse* (1606), the lexicographer Jean Nicot alludes to the above passage from Du Fouilloux in the following entry: "*Basset.* Is a breed of earth-dog (*chien terrien*), low-mounted on crooked legs and short-haired (although there is another variety, shaggy like water-dogs and straight-legged), that go to earth after foxes and badgers in order to slay them, or hold them at bay until they are dug out with forks, borers, pincers, hoes, and shovels...Le Fouilloux, in his book on hunting, Chapter 60, opines that the breed of such dogs originated in the regions of Flanders and Artois in France, on account of which they are sometimes called *chiens d'Artois*. They are also called *chiens terriers*, because they go to earth in the underground burrows and dens of badgers (*Taissons*) and foxes."

Turberville's translation now continues:]

And bycause it is good pastime, and brave fight, without great payne or travayle to the huntesman, therefore I have thought good to set downe here some precepts for the **entryng of Terriers** [*dresser les Bassetz*], and for the better **fleshying** [*mettre à la chair*: rewarding with the flesh of game killed] and encouragyng of them.

You shall beginne to entre them assoone as they be eight or tenne Months old: For if you entre not a **Terrier** before he be a yeare old, you shall hardly ever make him take to earth. And you must take good heede that you encourage them, and rebuke them not at firste: nor that the Foxe or Badgerd do hurte them within the earth, for they will never love the earth agayne. And therefore never entre a yong **Terryer** in an earth where there is an olde Foxe or Badgerd: But firste lette them be well entred, and be a yeare old full or more. You shall do well also to put in an olde **Terryer** before them which may abide and endure the furie of the Foxe or Badgerd. You may entre them and fleshe them in sundrie ways. First when Foxes and Badgerds have yong Cubbes, take all your olde **Terryers** and **put them into the grounde** [*les laisser aller en terre*]: and then they beginne to bay (which in the earth is called Yearnyng), you muste hold your yong **Terryers** every

one of them at a sundry hole of some angle or mouth of the earth, and they may herken and heare theyr fellowes yearne. And when you have taken the old Foxes and Badgerdes, and there is nothing left in the earth but the yong Cubbes, take out then all your old **Terryers**, and couple them up: then put in your yong **Terryers** and encourage them crying, "To him, To him, To him" [*les hardissant en terre, en criant: "Coule à luy Basset, Coule à luy, hou, prenez prenez"*]: and if they take any yong Cubbe, **lette them take theyr pleasure of him, and kill him within the grounde** [*il leur faut laisser estrangler dedans la tranchee ou pertuis*]: and beware that the earth fall not downe upon them and smoother them. **That done, take all the rest of the Cubbes and Badgerd pigges home with you, and frie theyr livers and theyr bloud with cheese, and some of theyr own greace, and thereof make your Terryers a rewarde, shewyng them always the heads and skinnes to encourage them.** [*Ce fait, faudra porter tous les petits Tessoneaux et Regnardeaux au logis, & en faire fricasser les foyes & le sang, avecques du fromages, & de la graisse, puis leur en faire curée, en leur monstrant la teste de leur gibier.*] When they have been rewarded or rather before, washe them Sope and warme water to get out the clay whiche shall be clodded in theyr heare: for els they will soone become mangie: and that would be hard to be cured. You may entre them also thus: you must take old Foxes and Badgerdes alive with your old **Terryers** and **the help of such clampes and holdfastes** [*avec des tenailles propices à ce faire*] as you shall see here portrayed: Take them and cut away theyr nether Jawe wherin **there wang teeth** [*les grands crochets*] be set, and never touch the upper Jawe, but let it stande to shewe the furie of the Beast, although it can do no hurte therwith: **then make an earth in some of your closes** [*faire des terres en vn pré*], and make it large inough, bycause that the **Terryers** may fight and turne therein the better, and that they may go in twoo together: then cover the burowe or earth with bordes and turnes, and put the Foxe or Badgerde therein: then put in al your **Terryers** both yong and old and encourage them with wordes, as hath bene before declared, and as the Arte requyreth: and when they have yearned sufficiently, then beginne to digge with spades

and mattocks to encorage them against such tyme as you must use to digge over them: then take out the Foxe or Badgerde with the clampes or pinches, killyng it before them, or lette a **Greyhounde** [*Leurier*] kill it in their sight, and make them reward thereof. It shall be well to cast them some bread or cheese upon the vermin assoone as it is dead, for the better boldyng and encouragyng of them. If you will not cut the Jawe of the Foxe or Badgerd, then break out al his teeth that he bite not the **Terryers**, and it shall suffyze as well.

Chapter 66. Of the nature and properties of a Foxe and a Badgerd.

[Chapitre 61. Du naturel et complexion des Regnardz et Blereaux]

As you have two kyndes or more of every other chace by diversitie of names [*Tovt ainsi qu'il y a deux especes de Bassetz*]: so of these vermyne there are Foxes and their Cubbes, and Badgerdes and theyr Pigges *[il y a semblement deux especes de Tessons et de Regnardz]*: **the female of a Foxe is called a Bitche, and he himself a Doggefoxe** [*des Regnardz, de grands et petits Goupils*]: **the female of a Badgerde is called a Sowe, and the male a Badgerde or a Borepygge of a Badgerde** *[sçauoir est des Tessons, de Porchins, et de Chenins]*. **Yet some will not allowe this difference** [*Combien que plusieurs veulent dire, que les Tessons sont d'vne mesme sorte, et qu'il n'y a pointe de difference entre les Porchins et Chenins*]: but I can prove it by good reason and by diversities of colour, nature, and proportion. The **Badgerde pigges** [*Porchins*] at comming out of the earth do commonly make and cast their fyaunts [badger dung]: and they never do it untill they have made a hole in the earth with theyr snowte or with their foote: and then they fyaunt within it and hide it: this **Foxe Cubbes** [*Chenins*] do not. Also the Badgerde [*Porchins*] maketh his hole commonly in sande or light earth which is easy to digge, and in open places, to have comfort of the Sunne: for they sleepe uncessantly, and are much fatter than the Foxecubbes [*Chenins*] be...

[Turberville translation makes a total hash of the above passage, mistaking Du Fouilloux' two distinct varieties of badger for two sexes of the same variety.]

This subtletie they [Badgerdes] have, that when they perceive the **Terryers** beginne to yearne them, and to lye at

them, they will stoppe the hole betweene the **Terryers** and them, least the **Terryers** should follow them any further: and if then the **Terryers** baye still, they will **remove their baggage** [*remver leur menage*] with them, and go into another chamber or angle of their Burrowe...

All these thinges I have seene by experience: they are long lived, and harde to kyll. For I have seen a **well byting Greyhounde** [*de bons et forts Leuriers*], take a Badger and teare his guttes out of his bellye, and yet the Badgerd hath fought still, and would not yeeld to death. True it is that they are very tender upon the snowt, and you can not give them so little a blowe upon the snowte with a sticke, but they wil dye immediately.

...But sometimes they [Foxes] take a Badgers old Burrowe, which hath moe chambers, holes, and angles. When a good *Terryer* doth once reache a Foxe, they defende themselves shrewdly, but yet nothing like the Badgerde, neyther is their byting so daungerous.

Chapter 68. Of the nature of a Badger, out of the same Author.

The Badgerd (sayth he ["the same Author": namely, the unnamed Du Fouilloux]) maketh but slow speede before the hounds, and cannot long stand up. So that commonly she fighteth it out at the Baye, or else taketh the earth, and there is killed with **Terryers**. For if you finde a Badgerde abroad, it shall not be from its burrow lightly...Their biting is venomous, as the Foxes is, but they make better defence for themselves, and fight more stoutly, and are much stronger...The skynne of a Badgerd, is not so good as the Foxes, for it serveth for no use, unlesse it be to make myttens, or to dresse horscollers withall.

Chapter 69. The hunting of the Badgerd, out of the same Author.

He that would hunte a Badgerde, must seeke the earthes and burrowes where they be, and in a fair moonshine night, let him go unto them upon a cleare winde, and stoppe all the holes but one or two, and in those let him set sacks or pokes fastened with some drawing string which may shut him in as sone as he streineth the bag...The bagges or Sacks being thus set, let your Huntsman cast off hys Houndes, and beate all the groves, hedges, and tufts, within a mile or halfe a mile aboute, whiche are most likely: and when the Badgerd heareth any hunting, hee will straightwayes home to his earth, and there is taken as beforesayd...but if ye houndes chance to encounter him before he be gotten to his earth, or recovered near unto it, then wil he stand at bay like a Bore, and make you good pastime...

Chapter 71. Howe to digge for a Foxe or a Badgerde, and what instrumentes are meete for the same.

[*Chapitre 62. Comme il faut bescher et prendre les Regnardz et Tessons, et des instruments qu'il faut auoir pour ce faire.*]

They which will heare good pastime at a Foxe, or a Badgerd within the grounde [*Tous Seigneurs qui voudront exercer la chasse des Chiens de terre*], must be furnished with such tooles and appertinances as followe, and as are heare before this present chapter portrayed. First let there be in the company five or six strong fellowes which can well endure to dyg and delve. Next you must have **as many good and arant** [eager] **terriers** [*d'vne demye douzaine de bons Chiens de terre*], garnished with collers full of belles, to make the Foxe or Badgerd **start** [*s'acculent*] the soner, to save them from hurting. But when your **Terryers** are out of breath, or their Belles are stopped up and glutted with earth, or that you perceive the vermine is angled (which is to say, gone to the furdest parte of his chamber to stand at defence) then you may take off the collers: but at the first they serve to greate purpose, to make the vermine eyther start or angle...

[At this point, Turberville censors out most of the following passage from Du Fouilloux, corresponding to the above-described woodcut, which Turberville's version also omits to reproduce:

Further, to do the thing properly, the Seigneur must have his **little cart** [*petite charrette*], in which he will ride **with a young girl of sixteen to seventeen years of age, who will stroke his head along the way** [*avec la fillette aagée de seize à dix-sept ans, laquella luy frottera la teste par les chemins*]. He should have half a dozen rugs to throw on the ground **in order to listen to the bassets giving tongue** [*à fin d'escouter l'abboy des Bassetz*], or he should have a **pneumatic mattress** [*vn lict plein de vent*], which he can use in this manner...**The raves of the charrette** [*Toutes les cheuilles at paux de la charette*] should be hung with flasks and bottles, and at the end should be a wooden coffer **full of cold game fowls, hams, beef tongues, and other good throat-tackle** [*plein de coqs*

d'Inde froids, iambons, langues de bœuf, et autres bons harnois du gueule]. And in wintertime he can have have his little pavilion brought along in which a fire can be lit to warm him, or [*ou bien donner un coup en robbe à la Nymphe.*]

The instruments to digge withal must be these, sharp pointed **Spades** [*Tarieres*], round hollowed Spades, and flatte broade Spades, Howes, or **Mattocks** [*Pietes*], and Pickaxes, a **Colerake** [*Bezoches*] and a payr of **Clampes or Holdfasts** [*Tenailles*], **Shovells** [*Paesles*] both shodde and bare, an Axe and a sharpe paring Spade...:the clampes or holdfasts to take a Foxe or Badgerd out alive, wherewith you may make pastime afterwards, or to help the **terriers** when they are aferd to bite a vermine...You shall also have a Payle to set water unto your **Terriers** at suche times as they come out to take breath...And w^t these instruments and such like necessary implements a Lord or Gentleman may fill a prettie little Cart or Wagon made for ye purpose, ye which he may cause to be caried on the field with him, alwais provided that when the sayd cariage is loded, he forget not to cause his Cook and Butler to hang good store of bags and bottels about the raves and pinnes [rails and pegs] thereof, for it will be both comely and comfortable. **In this order of batell, a noble man or gentleman may march to besiege the Foxe and Badgerd, in their strongest holes and castles. And may breake their Casmats** [vaulted chambers under a rampart], **Platformes, Parapets, and work to them with Mynes, and countermines, untill they get their skynnes, to make furres and myttens.** [*Et faut que le Seigneur marche en bataille de ceste façon, equippé de tous les ferrements cy dessus mentionnez, à fin d'aller donner l'assaut aux gros Tessons et Vulpins en leur fort, et rompre leur chasmates, plocus, paraspets, et les auoir par mine, et cntre-mine, iusques au centre de la terre, pour en auoir les peaux à faire des carcans pour les arbalalestiers de Gascongne.*]

Chapter 72. Howe to enter your Terriers according to the ground, and how to trench and dig.

[*Comme on doit lascher les Bassetz selon les terres qu'on voit: Et ce qu'on doit faire pour bescher et miner les Tessons.*]

Before you put your **Terriers** into the ground, you must have consideration what kynd of mould [earth] it is, and marke well the situation thereof, and as neare as you can judge where aboutes the chiefe angles or chambers should be, or else you may worke cleane contrarie, and rather hinder the **Terriers** than further them. As if the earthe or burrowe, be hanging on a side of a banke, you shall do beste to put in your **Terriers** bylowe towardes the vale, to the end that you may digge to him with most ease...And when you have digged so long that you be come to the angle, then thrust your **spade** [*tariere platte*] betweene the **vermine** [*Tesson*] and the **terryer**, so that the vermine can not by any meanes come out upon your **Terrier**. For in some chamber you may chance to find five or six vermine together, which may hurt your poore terrier, and discourage him. When you have stopped them in thus, then work with your broad spades and other tooles, and make a large trench if you will have good sport, and put in your **Terryers** to the vermine, and you shall see bold fight of all fashions. You must take heed to the subtleties of the vermine, especially the Badgerds. For sometimes they will stop up the trench betwene them and the **Terriers**, and worke themselves further in, so that your **Terriers** shall not be able to find them, not to know what is become of them. Sometimes when you have found their *Casmat* and chiefe strength, you may take them out alive with your holdfasts or clampes, **and therein use this policie and foresight** [*mais il y a mystere à les prendre*]. Take them with your tongs or clampes by the lower chappe, the one clampe in the mouth, the other under the throate, and so drawe them out. For if you should take them out by the body or necke, they should have libertie to byte and snatch at the **Terryers**, which wil be doing with them as you take them out. Being thus taken, put them into a sacke or poke, to hunt with your **Terryers** in your gardens or close courtes, at your pleasure. He that will be present at such pastimes, may do well to be booted: For I have lent a Foxe or a

Badgerd ere nowe, a piece of my hose, and the skynne and fleshe for companie, which he never restored agayne. Let these fewe precepts suffise for the hunting of Foxes and Badgerds.

In 1582, Jean Feyerabendt printed *Newen Jagd und Weidwerck Buch* ("New Book of Hunting and the Chase") in Frankfurt. Contrary to the promise of its title, the text—by his brother, Sigismond Feyerabendt—is essentially just a translation of Du Fouilloux' *La Vénerie*. The accompanying woodcuts, on the other hand, are splendidly new, being the commission of the great Swiss engraver, Jost Ammon (1539-91). Although his woodcuts are far more artistically accomplished than those illustrating Du Fouilloux (1560), Ammon's version of Du Fouilloux' *charrette de chasse* woodcut depicts exceedingly odd-looking, pig-headed, bob-tailed earth-dogs that are low to the ground despite having legs of normal length only because the legs are made to flop fore-and-aft at double-jointed angles. In fact, we won't find a German pictorial representation of an earth-dog that looks anything like a basset or dachshund until over a century later (see below: Fleming, 1719).

•1682-86 Johann **Täntzer**: *Jagtgeheimnüsz.*

Täntzer's *Der Dianen Hohe und Niedere Jagtgeheimnüsz, darinnen die gantze Jagt-Wissenschafft Aussfuhrlich zu befinden* ("Higher and Lower Chase-Mystery of Diana, in which the whole Science of Hunting is thoroughly revealed"; where the "higher chase" of deer, boar, wolf, and bear was reserved exclusively to the king and his privileged circle; whereas the "lower chase" of inferior objects of sport such as the fox, badger, rabbit, and hare was permitted to the king's less exalted subjects), first published in German in Copenhagen in 4 volumes in 1682-86 (Schwerdt II, 245), ranks as one of the most popular hunting books of the seventeenth and eighteenth centuries. One of its fifty-nine copperplates depicts a dog identified by caption as a *"Dachs kriecher"* ("badger-crawler"), whose image Sanborn (*ibid.*, p. 17) describes as "that of a small, straight-legged terrier or ordinary cur with narrow, stiff, pointed ears and a tail like that of a pug crooked off to one side."

•**1685**   Christian Franz **Paullini**: *Cynographia curiosa*.

The second earliest attested occurrence of the word *Dachshund* appears in a little-known book published in only one edition in Nürnberg in 1685: *Cynographia curiosa seu canis descriptio ...et mantissa curiosa ejusdem argumenti, complectente Joh. Caji libell. de canibus Britannicis...* ("Cynological studies or the description of the dog...and supplementary studies on this same subject, including the essay of Johannes Caius on British dogs..."), written in Latin (with occasional German interpolations) by Christian Franz **Paullini** (1643-1711).

Paullini twice employs the word *Dachshund* in this work, both times in the section which describes the varieties of dogs [*differentia canum*] according to a dozen different criteria—such as country, size, form, and function. Under the heading of "Size", Paullini cites a passage in German prescribing a chemical technique for suppressing growth in puppies. In his scholarly monograph, *The Dachshund Handbook* (1950), Clifford L.B. Hubbard errs in stating that Paullini cites this passage with explicit reference to *Dachshunds*. In fact, the word *Dachshunds* appears nowhere under the heading of "Size" but rather under the quite separate heading of "Form":

> Certain dogs have monkey-like noses [*simos nasos*]. Certain dogs (smaller than the former and white) by reason of the fore-half of their hair mode assume the form of little lions, and are called on that account *Löwchen*. Certain among the hunting dogs [*venaticos*] have short legs and extremely long bodies [*brevissimas tibias et corpora longissima*], in order to go down into the deep lurking-places of wild animals; they are called *Dachshunds* [*Dachs-hunde dicuntur*].

Under the general heading of "Function", Paullini subdivides the functional varieties of dogs into House Dogs [*Domestici*], Farm Dogs [*Villatici*], Herding Dogs [*Pecuarii*], Hunting Dogs [*Venatici*], Tracking Dogs [*Vestigatores*], Coursing Dogs [*Vertragi*], Water Dogs [*Aquatici*], and Other Varieties [*Alii alius generis*]. In this last category, Paullini lists, without comment, *Dachshunds* [*Dachs-hüner*]—apparently forgetting that he was pleased to count them among the Hunting Dogs in the foregoing excerpt.

•**1719**   Hans von **Fleming**: *Der Vollkommene Teutsche Jäger*.

The first illustration bearing a caption that relates the pictorial representation of a dog to the word *Dachshund* appeared in *Der Vollkommene Teutsche Jäger, darinnen die Erde, Gebürge, Kraüter und Baüme, Wälder, Eigenschaft der Wilden Thiere und Vögel, so wohl historice, als physice, und anatomice: dann auch die behörigen Gross- und kleinen Hunde...* ("The Complete German Hunter, wherein is treated the Earth, Mountains, Thickets and Trees, Woods, Nature of the Wild Animals and Birds, Historical as well as Physical and Anatomical: then also the Appropriate Big and Small Dogs..."), published in two volumes in Leipzig in 1719 and 1724, written by Hans Friedrich **von Fleming**, largely after Johann Coler's *Oeconomia ruralis et domestica* (published in Wittenberg in 1593-99). One very crude illustration bearing the caption *"Tachs kriecher"* ("badger-crawler") depicts a dog with very short, bent legs; large, pendent ears; smooth coat; and gay, tapering tail—all features broadly congruent with those of the modern dachshund but so ill-drawn in a clumsy attempt at foreshortening as to be inconclusory. Another illustration bearing the caption *"Tachs krieger"* ("badger-fighter") depicts a dog with moderately short, straight legs; moderately short muzzle; small, pendent ears; smooth coat; and gay, tapering tail—somewhat resembling a modern Dachsbracke. In his text (as cited below), von Fleming explicitly employs the expression *"Dachs-hund"* as a synonym for the short-legged *"Tachs kriecher"*. The straight-legged *"Tachs krieger"* represented in

the plate is not mentioned in the body of von Fleming's text.

Of the short- and crooked-legged *"Tachs kriecher"*, von Fleming writes:

..the good God created special wild animals of various kinds that seek to hide their coverts underground; to which end one uses a special breed of small earth-dog [*kleinen Erdhündlein*] as a burrower [*Schliefer*] or crawler [*Kriecher*], which—for their better progress—are small, long and slender in body [*klein, lang, und schmal vom Leibe*] and furnished with low little feet somewhat bent in [*mit niedrigen etwas eingebogenen Füsslein*] and serviceable for burrowing. These pygmies, miners, or sappers [Pygmæi, *Bergleute, oder* Minirer] should properly be called the dwarfs of all other dogs, and are, although small, nevertheless exceedingly zealous and seek to perform their master's service to the utmost of their capacity: They crawl, drive, and track their quarry [*kriechen, treiben und stöbern ihr Wild*], give tongue and hold their game at bay [*schlagen an und stehen vor*], with truly such diligence and vigor as ever the other breeds, in order to indicate to the huntsman where the prey dwells. This dwarf-breed is usually colored red or blackish with pendent ears [*behangenen Ohren*] almost like a hound [*Jagd-hund*]—except that, as dwarves, they are smaller. When they are a year old, it is necessary that one bring them to the badger-burrow [*Dachs-Bau*] and cause an old trained dog to enter it: When the latter has found the prey, lies near to it, and gives tongue, the young dog must hear such and be encouraged thereto. When the badger has been dug out or caught alive in another way, his teeth must be punched out and he must be put into a trench covered over with boards and soil, in order that the little dog [*Hündlein*] be incited to crawl in and encouraged to slay it. So that this young dog might be all the more eager, he should not merely be encouraged by talking to him in friendly tones but he also should be made to feed on the given bloody corpse. These badger-dogs [*Dachs-hunde*] are occasionally used as trailers [*Stöber-Hunde*] after hares or foxes, to hunt them out at such times as they go to ground [*sich verkriechen*]; or to locate and dig out polecats and other vermin.

•**1738** Johann **Ridinger**: *Entwurff einiger Thiere.*

One of the eighteen skillfully executed copperplates in *Entwurff einiger Thiere, Theil 1 (von 7): Hunde* ("Sketch of some Animals, Part 1: Dogs"), by Johann Elias **Ridinger** (1698-1767), first published in Augsburg in 1738 (Schwerdt III, 141), depicts two types of dogs identified by caption as *"Tachs Schliefer"* ("badger burrower") and *"Tachs Würger"* ("badger slayer"). The Tachs *Würger* is represented as a powerfully compact, short-muzzled, long-haired dog with straight legs of normal length—looking rather like a long-haired version of the *Tachs Krieger* ("badger fighter") of von Fleming (1719, above).

Fitzinger (1867, below) lists Ridinger's *Tachs Würger* as a precursory synonym under his own "Der geradebeinige Dachshund (*Canis vertagus, rectipes*)"; and Ridinger's *Tachs-Schliefer* under his own "**Der zottige Dachshund** (*Canis vertagus, sericeus*)". Ridinger's *Tachs Schliefer* (a synonym for *Tachs Kriecher*, according to excerpt given above from von Fleming, *ibid.*) looks similar in most points to von Fleming's *Tachs Kriecher* ("badger crawler"), insofar as both are portrayed with short, bent legs; large, pendent ears; smooth coat; and gay, tapering tail. These features of Ridinger's *Tachs Schliefer* are broadly congruent with those of the modern dachshund, except that the legs of the former are longer and its muzzle is shorter.

•**1740** Jean-Baptiste **Oudry**: *Pehr, Count Tessin's Dachshund.*

The first conclusive pictorial representation of a modern Dachshund is a superb oil painting by Jean-Baptiste **Oudry** (1686-1755) entitled *Pehr, Count Tessin's Dachshund, with Dead Game and Rifle* (Nationalmuseum, Stockholm, No. 864: belonging to M. C.J. Tessin). As rendered by the foremost exponent of animal painting of the eighteenth century, Pehr is a perfect black-and-tan Smooth Dachshund, displaying—in addition to an expression of utmost charm and alacrity—all the standard points of the *normalgros kurzhaar* type as would prevail well into the

twentieth century (that is, with legs distinctly more crooked and skull slightly broader than fashionable today). Count Carl Gustaf Tessin (1695-1770) was a Swedish statesman who served as ambassador to Vienna shortly before being posted ambassador extraordinary at Versailles 1739-42, where he so delighted the court of Louis XV with his social brilliance and wit that he succeeded in engineering a rapprochement between Sweden and France after a rift of sixty years. Perhaps Count Tessin brought Pehr with him from Vienna to Paris; or perhaps he acquired the animal from a French source while in Paris. In any event, the ambassador's pet was accorded the honor in 1740 of sitting for the celebrated animal portraitist Oudry, who held the office of painter of the royal hunt by court appointment.

•1746   H.W. **Döbel**: *Jäger-Praktika.*

In *Jäger-Praktika* ("Practical Instructions for the Sportsman")—a handbook so enduringly popular that, almost a century after the original publication, an updated *Neueröffnete Jäger-Praktika* was still being published by a descendant of the author in 1828—H.W. *Döbel* writes of the *"Dachshund"* (as translated by Sanborn, 1937):

> Among all the dogs previously described, this is the smallest. Nevertheless he has to be the most courageous, since he has to go into the burrows and tunnels underneath the ground which are often so narrow that he can hardly squeeze himself into them. He is, however, so skillful in this work that he also knows how to find his way out. There are various kinds of these dogs, but I have found the best ones to be the black, chocolate, and red dogs, which have somewhat bent feet and which are not so large that they cannot turn themselves in the fox burrow. Before they reach the age of one year, they do not have much inclination to crawl into the burrow, and it is therefore a good thing to set them on tame cats (whereupon they begin to get bold) and also if possible on living foxes and badgers. A still better plan is to take a fox or badger, dig a trench in the ground and cover it with boards and earth, let the fox run in and then start the **Dachshunds** after him; in this way they get broken in and learn also how to crawl into the burrows

the next time. It is also a very good practice, if one knows where young foxes are to be found, to let the dogs go in , and then dig the foxes out in the presence of the dogs; in this way they learn to stick to their work. Although a good **Dachshund** will stick to his task and keep constantly in front of his game, there are others whose fault consists in crawling continually in and out of the burrow. It is a fault, since in the meantime the badger or the fox dig themselves in or change their position so that the dog cannot find them immediately; and after one has dug down a considerable distance it becomes necessary to start in again at another place. It is best to let them go to ground naturally; you cannot force them in, and if they are pushed in violently it makes them worse, with respect to going to ground. One great advantage when they drive out the foxes is that it is not necessary to dig. Other people let some of these dogs chase hares and foxes. This works especially well when they are kept off the hare and allowed to hunt only foxes and many a fox is shot over them. This works out well, too, in hare hunting; for the hare does not put a high estimate on the little dogs and moves along slowly ahead of them so that it is easy to shoot him. The burrows, if there are any, must be closed or a guard placed in front of them, so that if the fox tries to go to ground, the hunter can shoot him.

•1758   Louis-Jean-Marie **Daubenton**: "Description du Chien et de ses variétés" in Buffon: *Histoire naturelle du Chien: Histoire naturelle, générale et particulière,* vol. 10.

In the tenth volume, published in 1758 in Paris, of the encyclopedic series—*Histoire naturelle, générale et particulière avec la déscription du Cabinet du Roi* ("Natural history, general and particular including the description of the Museum of the King") (appearing in 44 quarto volumes 1749-1804)—undertaken by Georges-Louis Leclerc, comte de **Buffon** (1707-88), one of Buffon's collaborators, Louis-Jean-Marie **Daubenton** (1716-1800), describes the general anatomy and the varieties of the domestic dog in his essay: *Description du Chien et de ses variétés* ("Description of the Dog and its varieties"). Amongst the varieties, Daubenton describes and illustrates the *Bassets.*

Bassets

Two breeds are distinguished among the bassets [*bassets*]: one breed (Plate xxxv, figure 1) has four straight legs of normal conformation; the forelegs of the other bassets [figure 2] are bent outwards [*arquées en dehors*]; that is why the first breed are called "Bassets with straight legs" [*Bassets à jambes droites*], and the second breed "Bassets with crooked legs" [*Bassets à jambes torses*]. All these dogs have extremely short legs, whence came their name basset [*bas*,"low"; *-et*, diminutive suffix]: this feature constitutes the chief difference that distinguishes them from coursing dogs [*chiens courants*] (Plate xxxii) and from scenthounds [*braques*] (Plate xxxiii); for bassets have a long muzzle, a big head, pendent ears, and an extremely elongated body; but it would hardly appear longer than that of the coursing dogs and of the scenthound, if it were supported on legs as tall as those of these dogs. Bassets have ears less long and less large than those of the coursing dogs, and their muzzles are more pointed. These dogs are black, with spots of tan

color on the eyes, chest, and lower legs; or white; or mixtures of white, black, and tan. There are some dogs—such as the water-dogs [*barbets*], spaniels [*épagneuls*], pugs [*doguins*], etc.—that have naturally short legs; but it seems that this conformation is in the bassets a kind of natural defect [*vice de la Nature*], since their legs are not only hyper-short, but deformed and affected by a symptom most akin to the malady called rachitis [rickets]; for the bones of the "Bassets with crooked legs" [*Bassets à jambes torses*] are swollen and bent [*gonflés et courbes*], rather like those of sufferers of rachitis....

...The coursing dog [*Chien courant*], the scenthound [*Braque*], and the basset [*Basset*] are but one and the same breed of dogs...I have likewise grouped the "Basset with crooked legs" [*Basset à jambes torses*] with the ordinary basset [*Basset ordinaire*], because the defect in the legs of this dog come originally only from a malady similar to *rachitis*, by which some individuals have been afflicted, and of which they have passed on the consequence, which is the deformation of the bones, to their descendants....

Dimensions Table

	Bassets à j. droites	*Basset à j. torses*	[Dachshund*
Length of body (nose to anus)	27 inches	32 inches	32 inches
Height of forequarters	12 inches	12 inches	12 inches
Height of hindquarters	13 inches	14 inches	11 inches
Length of head (nose to occiput)	6 inches	8 inches	8 inches
Length of ears	5 inches	5 inches	5 inches
Circumference of chest	18 inches	20 inches	19 inches
Ground clearance of chest	6 inches	5 inches	3 inches
Ground clearance of belly	7 inches	6 inches	5 inches
Length of tail	10 inches	12 inches	10 inches
Length of forearm (elbow to wrist)	5 inches	5 inches	5 inches]

[* The dimensions shown here for the *Basset à jambes torses* and *Basset à jambes* droites are excerpted from Daubenton (1758) and recalculated from the old French measures (e.g., "2 pieds.1 pouce.4 lignes" equals 27 inches). The interpolated corresponding dimensions for the modern Dachshund are derived from the idealized profile figure that illustrates the KC Breed Standard, scaled for purposes of comparison to a 32-inch nose-to-anus body-length. As represented by this set of measurements, the modern Anglo-American Dachshund and eighteenth-century *Basset à jambes torses* are virtually identical in their proportions; the only significant differences being that the modern Dachshund is lower to the ground and the eighteenth-century Basset was higher in the hindquarters.]

•**1761** Carl von **Hoppe**: [*unattributed source cited by Sanborn, ibid., p. 23*].

Von **Hoppe** writes (as translated by Sanborn, *ibid.*): "[There are] **long-legged** and **short-legged Dachshunds** with both **straight** and **curved** legs, like the dogs that trail on the leash [*Leithunde*]."

•**1780** Gottfried F. **Riedel**: *Icones Animalium* (1780).

The earliest book illustration bearing the caption "Dachshund" was by Gottfried F. **Riedel**, a Dresden painter & miniaturist. His illustration of two Dachshunds appears in *Icones Animalium* (1780) above the caption "**Dachshunde** (*Canis vertagus*)". [The Linnaean binomial, *Canis vertagus*, is discussed below, under Fitzinger (1867).]

•**1793-1840** [from Herbert S. Sanborn: *The Dachshund or Teckel* (1937), *passim.*]

F. E. **Jester**, a high official of the Prussian State Forestry, in the first volume of *Über die kleine Jagd, zum Gebrauch angehender Jagdliebhaber* ("On Small-Game Hunting, for the Use of the Prospective Amateur Hunter"), published in Königsberg in **1793**-1808, describes the varieties of "Dachshund" and makes the first explicit reference to the "**Wire-haired Dachshund**".

The earliest extant use of the diminutive form of *Dachshund* is apparently by the Prussian State-Forester Georg Ludwig **Hartig** (1764-1837) who, in his *Lehrbuch für Jäger und die es werden wollen....* (published in two volumes in **1810**, Stuttgart), distinguishes smooth and wire-haired "*Dachsels*".

Von der **Borch** is the first (**1814**) to urge in print that a long head must be a criterion of the Dachshund breed.

In what is apparently the first reference (**1820**) to long-haired Dachshunds, Dietrich aus dem **Winckell** condemns the "long-haired" variety of Dachshund.

Dr. **Reichenbach** describes eight varieties of "*Dachshund*" in **1836**.

Under the "*Dachshund*" breed description in *Haarwildjagd* ("Furred-Game Hunting"), **Ziegler** makes the first mention (**1840**) of the presence of "*gelb*" ("yellow") coloration in the breed.

•**1867** Leopold Joseph Franz Johann **Fitzinger**: *Die Rassen des zahmen Hundes.*

In *Die Rassen des zahmen Hundes* ("The Breeds of the Domestic Dog"), published in Vienna in 1867, Dr. Leopold **Fitzinger** (1802-1884) lays out his taxonomic system for classifying all the breeds of dogs prevalent at the time of writing. Fitzinger assigns each dog breed in his system its German popular name; its Linnaean species name, often coined by Fitzinger; and an annotated list of foreign and obsolete names for the same breed. Of the twelve breeds that constitute his Dachshunds Group, Fitzinger considers only one to be an irreducibly independent breed: namely, his *krummbeinige Dachshund* ("crooked-legged Dachshund"). This breed—which Fitzinger identifies with the *Basset à jambes torses* described and illustrated by Daubenton (above)—is the precursor of the modern Standard Smooth Dachshund. His other eleven Dachshund breeds—including the precursors of the modern Standard Longhaired and Wirehaired Dachshund breeds—Fitzinger regards as having been derived by crossing the *krummbeinige Dachshund* with various other breeds, as follows:

Group III. Dachshunde (*Canes vertagi*)

1. Der krummbeinige Dachshund

["The crooked-legged Dachshund" (*krumm* means "crooked, twisted, bent, or awry")]

(**Canis vertagus**) [*Vertagus* is a name of uncertain derivation and dubious pertinence to the Dachshund. Three different etymologies have been proposed for *Vertagus*:

1) *Vertagus* is a corruption of 2nd-century Latin *vertragus*, from Celtic for "swift greyhound" (from Celtic intensive *ver* and *trag*, 'foot; first attested use *ante* AD 180 in Arrian's *Kynegetikos*: see below, Chapter 4). Modern extrapolation to creeping Dachshunds of a classical term for swift greyhounds would constitute an absurdity.

2) *Vertagus* is a corrupt participial form of *vertere* ("to turn") meaning "bent", in reference to the Dachshund's crooked front legs; or

3) *Vertagus* is a corrupt participial form of *vertere* ("to turn") meaning "turner", in reference to the acrobatic tumbling style of hare-hunting peculiar to the extinct English Tumbler dog (which was neither short-legged nor an earth-dog). This last is the etymological derivation first advanced by Johannes Caius *De Canibus Britannicis* (1570), translated by Abraham Fleming as *Of Englishe Dogges* (1576):

Among houndes the Tumbler called in latine *Vertagus*, is the last, which commeth of this worde Tumbler flowing first of al out of the French fountaine. For as we say Tumble so they say *Tumbier*, reserving one sense and signification, which comprehende under this worde *Vertere*, so that we see thus much, that Tumbler commeth of *Tumbier*...This sorte of Dogges, which compasseth by

craftes, fraudes, subtleties and deceiptes, we Englishe men call Tumblers, because in hunting they turne and tumble, winding their bodyes in circle wise, and then fearcely and violently venturing upon the beast [hare], doth soddenly gripe it, at the very mouth of their receptacle, or closets before they can recover meanes, to save or succour themselves...Then having caught his pray he [the Tumbler or *Vertagus*] carryeth it speedily to his Master, wayting his Dogges returne in some convenient lurcking corner. These dogs are somewhat lesser than the houndes, and they be lancker & leaner, beside that they be somewhat prick eared. A man that shall marke the forme and fashion of their bodyes, may well call them mungrell Grehoundes if they were somewhat bigger.

In *The Gentleman's Recreation* (1674), Nicholas Cox modernizes A. Fleming's translation of Caius without attribution to either:

> The word Tumbler undoubtedly had its derivation from the French word Tumbier, which signifies to Tumble; to which the Latin name agrees, Vertagus, from Vertere, to turn; and so they do: for in hunting they turn and tumble, winding their Bodies about circularly, and then, fiercely and violently venturing on the Beast, suddenly gripe it at the very mouth of their Holes, before they can make any entrance for self-security...These Dogs are somewhat lesser than Hounds, being longer, leaner, and somewhat prick-eared. By the form and fashion of their Bodies they may be called Mongrel Grey-hounds, and justly, if they were somewhat bigger.]

Beagle terriar. *Anglorum.* Spelman. Glossar. archaiol. [Sir Henry Spelman *Glossarium archaiologicum* (**1626**).]

Turnspit. Cajus. De Canib. Brittan. [Johannes Caius *De Canibus Britannicis* (1570), translated by Abraham Fleming (1576): "A certaine dogge..when any meate is to bee roasted they go into a wheele...turning rounde about with the weight of their bodies...whom the popular sort hereupon call Turnespets."]

Vertagus, a **Tumble.** Rajus. Synops. quadrup. [John Ray (1628-1705) *Synopsis methodica Animalium Quadrupedum et Serpentini Generis* (1693). See *Canis vertagus* above.]

Basset à jambes torses. Buffon. Hist. nat. [Georges-Louis Leclerc, comte de Buffon (1707-88) *Histoire naturelle du Chien: Histoire naturelle, générale et particulière* (**1758**): vol. 10 of *Histoire naturelle, générale et particulière avec la déscription du Cabinet du Roi* (appearing in 44 quarto volumes, 1749-1804).]

Dachshund mit auswerts gebogenen Füssen. Haller. Naturg. Thiere. [Albrecht von Haller (1708-1777) *Naturgeschichte den Thiere.*]

Canis familiaris vertagus. Linné. Syst. nat. [Carl von Linnaeus (1707-1778) *Systema naturae* (**1758**).]

Turnspit. Penn. Synops. Quadrup. [Thomas Pennant (1726-1798) *Synopsis of Quadrupeds* (**1771**).]

Krumbeinigter Dachshund. Martini. Buffon Naturg. d. vierf. Thiere. [Friedrich Heinrich Wilhelm Martini (1729-1778) *Naturgeschichte der vierfüssigen Thiere*, translation of Buffon *Histoire naturelle des Quadrupèdes*; wherein *"Krumbeinigter Dachshund"* translates *"Basset à jambes torses ".*]...

The crooked-legged Dachshund [*krummbeinige Dachshund*] is one of those forms among the dogs that cannot be derived from any others and thus is treated as an independent dog-breed. It appears to have originated in the higher mountain ranges of Southern and Middle Europe, in particular the Pyrenees and Alps.

[Fitzinger's *krummbeinige Dachshund* is a precursor of the modern Standard Smooth Dachshund.]

2. Der geradebeinige Dachshund

["straight-legged Dachshund"]

(Canis vertagus, rectipes)

[*rectipes* means "straight-footed"; which would accord ill with a meaning for *vertagus* of "crooked-legged".]

Tumbler. Cajus. [op. cit. (**1576**).]

Vertagus, a Tumbler. Rajus [op. cit. (**1693**).]

Tachs-Würger. Ridinger. Entw. einiger Thiere. [op. cit. (**1738**).]

Basset à jambes droites. Buffon. [op. cit. (**1758**).]

Dachshund mit geraden Schenkeln. Haller. [op. cit.]

Turnspit. Penn. [op. cit. (**1771**).]

Dachs mit geraden Beinen. Martini. [op. cit.: wherein *"Dachs mit geraden Beinen"* translates *"Basset à jambes droites ".*]...

The straight-legged Dachshund [*geradebeinige Dachshund*] was very probably derived by crossing the crooked-legged Dachshund [*krummbeinige Dachshund*] with the German scenthound [*deutsche Stöberhund* aka *Canis sagax, venaticus irritans*].

[Fitzinger's *geradebeinige Dachshund* is probably a precursor of the modern Standard Wirehaired Dachshund.]

3. Der schweinschwänzige Dachshund

["pig-tailed Dachshund"]

(Canis vertagus syosurus)

[First attestation, 19th c.]

"The pig-tailed Dachshund [*schweinschwänzige Dachshund*] appears to have been derived by crossing the crooked-legged Dachshund [*krummbeinige Dachshund*] with the straight-legged Dachshund [*geradebeinige Dachshund*]."

[Fitzinger's *schweinschwänzige Dachshund* is extinct.]

4. Der rauhe Dachshund

["rough-haired Dachshund"]

(Canis vertagus, hirsutus)

[First attestation, 19th c.]

[According to Fitzinger, the rough-haired Dachshund was probably derived by crossing the straight-legged Dachshund (*geradebeinige Dachshund*) with the rough-haired Pinscher (*rauhe Pintsch* aka *Canis extrarius, hispanicus hirsutus*).]

[Fitzinger's *rauhe Dachshund* is probably a precursor of the modern Standard Wirehaired Dachshund.]

5. Der zottige Dachshund

["shaggy Dachshund"]

(Canis vertagus, sericeus)

Tachs-Schlieffer. Ridinger. Entw. einiger Thiere. [op. cit. (1738)]...

[According to Fitzinger, the rough-haired Dachshund was certainly derived by crossing the crooked-legged Dachshund (*krummbeinige Dachshund*) with the standard silky-haired dog (*grosse Seidenhund* aka *Canis extrarius*).]

[Fitzinger's *zottige Dachshund* is probably a precursor of the modern Standard Longhaired Dachshund.]

6. Der langhaarige Dachshund

["long-haired Dachshund"]

(Canis vertagus, longipilis)...

Canis familiaris vertagus, Var. c. Linné. Syst. nat. [op. cit. (1758)]...

[According to Fitzinger, the long-haired Dachshund was probably derived by crossing the crooked-legged Dachshund (*krummbeinige Dachshund*) with the standard poodle (*grosse Pudel* aka *Canis extrarius, aquaticus*).]

[Fitzinger's *langhaarige Dachshund* might be parental to the modern Standard Longhaired Dachshund.]

7. Der Roll-Dachshund

["carting Dachshund"]

(Canis vertagus, lasiotus)

[First attestation, 19th c.]

[According to Fitzinger, the carting Dachshund was probably derived by crossing the long-haired Dachshund (*langhaarige Dachshund*) with the shepherd dog (*Schafhund* aka *Canis domesticus, pastoreus*).]

[Fitzinger's *Roll-Dachshund* is extinct.]

8. Der gefleckte Dachshund

["variegated Dachshund"]

(Canis vertagus, varius)

Basset à jambes torses. Buffon. Hist. nat. [op. cit. (1758)]...

[According to Fitzinger, the variegated Dachshund was probably derived by crossing the crooked-legged Dachshund (*krummbeinige Dachshund*) with the pointer (*Vorstehhund* aka *Canis sagax, venaticus major*).]

[Fitzinger's *gefleckte Dachshund* is probably a precursor of the modern dappled Standard Smooth Dachshund.]

9. Der doppelnasige Dachshund

["double-nosed Dachshund"]

(Canis vertagus, nasica)

[First attestation, 19th c.]

[According to Fitzinger, the double-nosed Dachshund was probably derived by crossing the crooked-legged Dachshund (*krummbeinige Dachshund*) with the double-nosed bulldog (*doppelnasige Bullenbeiser* aka *Canis molossus, palmatus*).]

[Fitzinger's *doppelnasige Dachshund* is extinct.]

10. Der bunte Dachshund

["varicolored Dachshund"]

(Canis vertagus, pictus)

[First attestation, 19th c.]

[According to Fitzinger, the varicolored Dachshund was probably derived by crossing the crooked-legged Dachshund (*krummbeinige Dachshund*) with the roquet mastiff (*Roquet* aka *Canis molossus, fricator hybridus*).]

[Fitzinger's *bunte Dachshund* is extinct.]

11. Der gestreifte Dachshund

["striped Dachshund"]

(Canis vertagus, striatus)

[First attestation, 19th c.]

[According to Fitzinger, the striped Dachshund was probably derived by crossing the crooked-legged Dachshund (*krummbeinige Dachshund*) with the common mastiff (*gemeine Dogge* aka *Canis molossus, mastivus*).]

[Fitzinger's *gestreifte Dachshund* is extinct.]

12. Der Domingo-Dachshund

["Dominick-Dachshund"]

(Canis vertagus, dominicensis)

[First attestation, 19th c.]

[According to Fitzinger, the striped Dachshund was probably derived by crossing the crooked-legged Dachshund (*krummbeinige Dachshund*) with the tiger dog (*Tigerhund* aka *Canis leporarius, danicus corsicanus*).]

[Fitzinger's *Domingo-Dachshund* is extinct.]

The Dachshund is a terrier.

"A terrier!" bellows outraged Reason. "You just dragged us through nine yards of proof that the Dachshund is a basset. Now you want it should be a terrier? What kind of chimerical cockapoo is this? A Dachshund is a Dachshund is a Dachshund. Period."

"We couldn't agree more," soothes the author with nasal piety. "We would be the first to take up righteous cudgels against any heretic who would deny that a Dachshund is a Dachshund is a Dachshund. But have we not truly shown that the Dachshund is also a basset? And may we not in fairness be allowed to try to show that it is a terrier, too? Like good old terriers, then, let us forbear to enter the third compartment of the tripartite mystery of the Dachshund's doghood until all but one of the entrances has been stopped up. We will show that the several ancient breeds long held to be Dachshunds were nothing of the kind; and we will we show the Dachshund verily to be a terrier."

It is a commonplace of the Dachshund literature that medieval and classical art and writing abound in representations of long-bodied, short-legged hunting dogs. Inspection of those references actually cited, however, reveals that none of them prior a painting by Pisanello done around 1450 (see below) explicitly refers to the attributes of long body and short legs. In all these instances, extrapolation from modern preconceptions has been allowed to color interpretation of ancient sources.

The error of this type most commonly encountered in the Dachshund literature is the unwarranted extrapolation of an ancient dog's unknown body-form

from its working function by analogy with the body-form of some modern breed that has been developed to perform the same sort of work. A case in point is an eighth-century literary source entitled *Lex Bajuvariorum*, which contains an allusion to a particular variety of earth-dog that is couched exclusively in terms of its work as a beaver hunter. Many Dachshund writers have trotted out this eighth-century beaver-dog as a long-bodied, short-legged progenitor of the Dachshund. Yet the *Lex Bajuvariorum* itself says nothing about the appearance of the beaver-dog. As a matter of historical fact, not until the sixteenth century would long body and short legs first be mentioned as attributes of certain earth-dogs.

The *Lex Bajuvariorum* ("Law of the Bavarians")—a body of early Germanic laws largely derived from the fifth-century code of the Visigoths—was compiled shortly after 743, when Odilo duke of Bavaria unsuccessfully revolted against the Carolingian suzerainty of Carloman and Pepin the Short. The pertinent ordinance in the *Lex Bajuvariorum* (Tit. XIX, ¶ 4) in its entirety reads: *De eo cane, quem bibarhunt dicunt, qui sub terra venatur, qui occideret, reddat, et cum VII solid. componat.* This passage may be translated: "Of that dog, which they call *bibarhunt*, which hunts

The Dirt on Dachshunds and Terriers

underground: whosoever shall have killed [one], shall be obliged to make restitution, and to pay compensation of seven pieces of silver."

No direct information is given in this ordinance as to the physical appearance of the eighth-century Bavarian *bibarhunt*—in particular, as to whether it was short-legged like the modern Dachshund. Nor can the wording of the ordinance be construed as supplying any indirect clues as to the appearance of the *bibarhunt*—as we shall endeavor to show in the following digression on the meanings and implications of the ordinance's key phrases: "*bibarhunt*" and "*qui sub terra venatur*".

Bibarhunt is archaic Elbe Germanic for "beaver-dog" (the modern German equivalent is *Biberhund*). The *bibarhunt* hunted beaver. Until the twelfth century, the beaver (*Castor fiber*) was hardly less common in Europe—with a geographic distribution extending across Scandinavia, Britain, France, Germany, Eastern Europe, as far east as Siberia and as far south as Italy and Spain—than it would continue to be in North America until the nineteenth century. It is an index of the former abundance of the European beaver that over two hundred place-names in Germany contain some variation of the root-word *Biber*.

After the twelfth century, however, burgeoning commerce in various of its body parts—its pelt (a fashionable fur for hats and stoles); its scent-gland secretion (*castoreum*, a prized ingredient in medieval drugs that was believed until Claude Perrault's dissections of 1731 to be contained in the beaver's testicles, which— according to Pliny, Book VIII, ¶ 62—the beaver "tore off when he saw himself pursued by hunters to abandon as a ransom"); and its tail (deemed a liturgical "fish" fit for Lenten consumption on account of its "scales" and natatory use)—doomed the beaver to increasing rarity throughout medieval Europe. On Britain, the beaver was extirpated by the twelfth century. On mainland Europe, the

subspecies of Old World beaver evaded complete extinction only in a few shrinking enclaves in the Rhône, Elbe, and Vistula drainages. In Bavaria itself, the last indigenous beaver was killed in 1850.

The eighth-century *Law of the Bavarians* states that the *bibarhunt* "hunts underground" (*sub terra venatur*). This phrase is elliptical, insofar as it elides the subaquatic phase of the *bibarhunt's* subterranean hunting activity. The approach of the *bibarhunt* to the den of its semiaquatic quarry was governed by the unusual geometry of the den's entrance. Unlike the badger, the beaver does not enter its den simply by popping down a dry hole in the ground. Rather, the beaver swims out to the middle of its private pond, dives down to an underwater entrance, and crawls up a submerged tunnel into the heart of its armored island sanctuary.

A beaver family unit constructs such elaborate outworks for its den not by a single flurry of badgerly excavation but as the end-product of a subtle and cumulative engineering cycle that lifts its den ever higher by hydraulic stages. The proverbial beaver work ethic might indeed be said to be driven by the upward mobility of its den. First, the beavers burrow convergent tunnels upward into the alluvial soil of a watercourse bank, beginning below the waterline and terminating in a subterranean den above the water table; then they build a dam downstream; then they extend the burrows and den upward in pace with the rising pond in order to keep the den above the water table; then they roof over the den with an impenetrable mud-and-wattle armor as it approaches the ground surface; and on the foundation of this late roof, finally, the busy beavers heap up an artificial island of mud-and-wattle to house the ultimate den that succeeds the flooding of the last earthen den. The only way into this ultimate den remains the initial earthen tunnel—now completely water-filled.

To "hunt underground", then, the *bibarhunt*

must have had to swim deep underwater to the earthen tunnel entrance; crawl up the water-filled tunnel into the lightless den; and there kill or rout the beaver family. Beavers are formidable an-tagonists in a close fight with a dog. Von Hohberg (*ibid.*) wrote of beavers: "They can do great injuries to such dogs as might crawl into their earths by slashing upwards like wild sows. If a living beaver is confined alone in a barrel, so quickly does he manage to chop through it that no other animal can do likewise so easily."

On account of its amphibious work environ-ment, the *bibarhunt* might reasonably be supposed to have embodied a compromise between certain physical features appropriate to a water-dog and others befitting an earth-dog. As an earth-dog, the *bibarhunt* must have been fairly small. But would it also have been short-legged? Although short legs might help in negotiating the tunnel, they would ill serve in negotiating the water barrier. Certainly, no modern breed of water-dogs has short legs. On the contrary, today's extremely short-legged breeds rate as the poorest swimmers in dogdom. On mechanical grounds, it is quite unlikely that the aquatic *bibarhunt* resembled the modern Dachshund in respect of its extreme short-leggedness. On the other hand, the *bibarhunt* could have possessed normal length of leg without mechanical compromise to its effectiveness as an earth-dog.

What pictorial evidence survives of the appearance of the medieval *bibarhunt*? Von Hohberg (*ibid.*) illustrates his chapter about the beaver (Ch. 118) with a plate depicting the hunting of beaver in a pond. Dogs are both running along the bank and swimming in pursuit of two submerged beavers that the human hunters are try to spear and net from the bank. These *Biber-hunde* are medium-sized, short-haired, pendent-eared hounds whose legs are of normal length.

Suggestive as this baroque pictorial evidence is, it does not tell us conclusively what the medieval *bibarhunt*

looked like. First, it is possible that the *Biber-hunde* figured in this illustration are not earth-dogs at all and therefore not comparable to medieval *bibarhunt*. Von Hohberg (*ibid.*) writes in his chapter about the otter:

Otters have their burrows and dens in the bank next to the water; there with little Burrow- and Otterdogs [*mit kleinen Schlieff- und Otterhunden*] they are tracked down, driven out, and caught...No sooner does the hunter cause the dogs go to earth than he and his retainers enclose the burrow with a net and kill the otters with forks, spears, and hackers...Sometimes beavers and otters are also caught with dogs and nets. One must seek them out with dogs, allowing the dogs to track up and down the length of the water.

Von Hohberg here distinguishes two methods of hunting beaver or otter with dogs: by one, the dogs go to earth; by the other, the dogs pursue along and in a open body of water. In all likelihood, the second method used different dogs than the first. The second—open-water—method of hunting is plainly the subject of the plate illustrating von Hohberg's chapter on beaver; the dogs shown in it might be expected to be quite different in appearance from the earth-dogs (*kleine Schlieffhunde*) used in the first method.

An even more patent objection to extrapolating the appearance of the early medieval *bibarhunt* from von Hohberg's baroque *Biberhund* is raised by the great gap in time between the two. This millennial gap defies bridging, as no medieval descriptions or illustrations of beaver-hunting are known to have survived.

Illustrations have survived, however, of the medieval *otter-dog*. Since the beaver and the otter are both web-footed, flat-tailed amphibious mammals of compar-able body length that live in subterranean dens dug into river banks from underwater entrances, it might be expected that the appearance of the medieval otter-dog would provide a plausible clue to the appearance of the

medieval beaver-dog. The "Otter-dogge" is first attested by name about 1175, during the reign of Henry II of England. An illumination in the French manuscript in the Bibliothèque Nationale de France entitled *Le livre du Roy Modus et de la Royne Racio le quel fait mençion commant on doit deviser de toutez manières de chasses* ("The book of King Measure and Queen Calculation which explains how to organize all kinds of hunting")—written in 1379 by Henri de Ferrières—depicts three otter-dogs at work coursing a submerged otter along the banks and in the shallows of a stream while hunters jab the otter with long forks. These three dogs are big, long-legged hounds—similar in build to the modern English Otterhound and very dissimilar to the modern Dachshund.

Medieval otterdogs are also depicted at work in a miniature in a nearly contemporaneous treatise, entitled alternatively *Le Livre de la chasse* ("The Book of the Hunt") or *Miroir de Phébus, des deduicts de la chasse des bestes sauvaiges et des oyseaux de proie* ("Mirror of Phoebus, of the pleasures of the hunt of wild beasts and game birds"), written in 1387 by Gaston III Phébus (1331-1391), comte de Foix (a countship in the foothills of the Pyrenees). The most beautiful of the manuscripts of *Miroir de Phébus* is

the lavishly and instructively illuminated product of the atelier of the Bedford Master in Paris from the first quarter of the fifteenth century, preserved in the Bibliothèque Nationale. A leading exponent of the International Style, the Bedford Master is noted for his sedulous and naturalistic treatment of rustic details as a counterpoint to the artificiality of the courtly pursuits depicted in his paintings. The Bedford Master's narrative use of genre vignettes strongly reflects the work of contemporary panel painting masters in Flanders.

The miniature in question—entitled *Comment on doit chasaer et prendre la loutre* ("How to hunt and take otter")—shows five otter-dogs variously occupied: three

are scent-tracking on the banks of a stream; one is investigating a hollow tree trunk; and one is swimming in pursuit of a submerged otter into which hunters on the banks are thrusting spear and trident. All five otter-dogs are—like those depicted in *Livre du Roy Modus*—big, long-legged, short-muzzled, pendent-eared hounds that could scarcely look less like modern Dachshunds.

Nevertheless, the patent dissimilarity between these late medieval otter-dogs and the modern Dachshund does not necessarily imply that the early medieval *bibarhunt* was equally dissimilar to the modern Dachshund. For the *bibarhunt* of *Lex Bajuvariorum* was an earth-dog (hence appropriate to the first of the two methods of otter- and beaver-hunting as distinguished by von Hohberg, above); whereas the otter-dogs represented in these late medieval manuscripts are clearly engaged in the second—namely, open-water—method of otter- or beaver-hunting.

That none of the dogs represented in these two late medieval miniatures of otter-hunting were employed therein as earth-dogs is confirmed by the associated text of the manuscript in which Gaston Phébus describes the use of dogs in hunting otter:

How to hunt and take otter. [*Comment on doit chaeser et prendre le Loutre.*]

> When the hunter wishes to hunt otter, he should have scenthounds [*Limiers*] and should send out four hunt servants [*valets*] tracking, two upstream and the other two downstream...: and if there is otter in the area, one pair or the other will come across evidence of it: for the otter cannot always stay in the water but comes ashore in the night, in order to void itself and graze on the grass [*pour soy vuyder et paistre de l'herbe*: n.b. otters are in fact strictly carnivorous], which it does at no other time. And if his dog picks up the scent [*et si son Chien encontre*], the hunter should look about whether he can see its tracks, either in the sand or in other soft ground near the water, and should examine which way they head, whether upstream

or down. And if he cannot verify its presence by spoor [*le pied*], he ought to verify its presence by otter excrement [*les fiantes ou espraintes*], and put his dog upon the otter's drag [scent-trail], or turn the otter as one does a stag or boar. And if the dog is unable to pick up or follow the otter's drag from that spot, it may be given leeway to go running a league (a mile-and-half) up- or downstream, for an otter often goes foraging half a league at a time...And should it become necessary to mount a hunting party for the otter, then, just as for the stag...the hunter should have his dogs leashed and ordered and disposed [*aura veu et diuisé et desieuné ses Chiens*], between those that will turn the otter and those that will close with it...And the scenthound-handler with the his dogs ought always to search the banks and the roots near the water until one of the dogs finds it [*Et le **valet du limier** et des autres doiuent tousioiurs querir par les riues et racines pres de l'eau, iusques à tant que l'vn des Chiens le trouuent*]. And there ought to be two or three hunt servants upstream where the scenthound-handler will come across them, and as many again downstream in a place where the water is shallowest: and each should have a pitchfork [*son baston fourché*]: and face forward attentively. And when he will see the otter coming in front of him, which will be coming beneath the water, he should spear if he can; or otherwise when it will have passsed either upstream or downstream, he should run along the stream to another place where there is shallow water, and await

it, to see again if he can spear it. And such ought to be done, as many times as necessary to spear it: for if the dogs are good for otter, they will come always hunting and searching out the banks under the roots, and thus it is a certainty that either the dogs will take it, or that the people will spear it [*car si les Chiens sont bons pour la Loutre, viendront tousiours chassant et querant apres les riues dessous les racines, et ainsi ne pourra il estre que les Chiens ne le prennent, ou que les gens ne le fierent*]. And this makes a bonny lark of a hunt...when the dogs are good, and the streams are little. But if the streams are big, or it is a fishpond or a pond [*vn viuier ou vn estang*], one should have nets that stretch from one bank to the other, weighted on the bottom, and not on the top, so that the net will go to the bottom of the water. And two men should hold the ends in both hands, one man on one

bank, the other on the opposite bank. And when the otter coming along underwater endeavors to pass, it will run against the net, and the men will feel the tug in the end of the rope that they are holding and ought to pull in their net [*Et quand le Loutre qui viendra dessous l'eau cuidera passer, il s'en viendra bouter au filet, et ils sentiront bransler le bout de la corde qu'ils tendront s'ils doiuent tirer leur filet*]. And thus will otter best be taken. The dogs that are good for otter, if one puts them to stag, are marvelously good as long as they're not too old.

The foregoing excerpt explicitly identifies the dogs specially used in otter-hunting as *limiers* (from OF *liem* or *lien*, "leash"), meaning "leash-hounds" or "trackers". The medieval *limier* was a large, powerful, long-legged, short-haired, short-muzzled, pendent-eared, loose-lipped hound of the of St. Hubert stamp—not less prized by the royal stag- and boar-hunter for its swiftness than for its keenness of nose. As solitary tracker and attacker of fleeing quarry, the *limier* was quite distinct in form and function from the *piqueurs de la meute* (long-muzzled, erect-eared, tuck-loined, smooth-haired packhounds), which set in a mob upon bayed quarry at the terminus of its flight.

The form and function of the *limier* persisted unchanged for centuries after Gaston Phébus. *Limiers* indistinguishable from those in *Miroir de Phébus* are extensively depicted (Ch. 29 & 45) and described by Du Fouilloux (1560) in connection with the stag hunt. Indeed, the word *limier* is retained and extended in modern French, referring not only to any of the large modern scenthounds but also colloquially to the human breed of sleuths and police inspectors.

The Old French word *limier* was assimilated into English in Chaucer's time as *limer*, *lymer*, or *lyemmer* but fell into abeyance (except as an heraldic term) by the end of the seventeenth century. Caius (1570) lists the *Lyemmer* as one of his seven classes of noble British hunting dogs, placing it midway between the Harrier (by virtue of its nose) and the Greyhound (by virtue of its speed).

The foregoing excerpt from Gaston Phébus' text on otter-hunting proves that the dogs used in medieval otter-hunting were *limiers* whose jobs in the otter-hunt included trailing, turning, investigating riparian tree-roots, and taking the otter in the water—but not going to earth. The textual excerpt also teaches us that the various activities depicted in the Bedford Master's otter-hunt miniature should be interpreted by the viewer not as happening simultaneously but consecutively. Like a comic strip liberated from the chronological discipline of the horizontal strip, this miniature must be read as a four-dimensional palimpset of successive events that occur in an implicit narrative sequence within the framed space.

Gaston Phébus' text on the otter-hunt enables the viewer of the otter-hunt miniature to order its component vignettes in narrative sequence. First, the *limiers* and their *valets* search for the otter's drag on the banks of the watercourse; then they find it and follow it toward the otter; then the alarmed otter pops down its vent inside the hollow tree and out into the water; then

the dogs spot it swimming underwater and splash after it in pursuit; then servants stationed on the banks try to impale the submerged otter as it passes.

By such a reading of the miniature, it is not implausible that the two sandy-colored otter hounds on the far bank—one scent-trailing on the ground; the other poking his head into a hollow tree trunk—represent one and the same otter hound: first following the otter's drag and then driving the alarmed otter down its vent hole inside the hollow tree and out into the stream. Similarly, the two grey-colored otter hounds—one scent-trailing on the near banks; the other swimming in pursuit of the otter—might represent the same individual in successive activities.

There are modern analogues to these medieval otter hounds. Descended from the same medieval French hound stock as the modern Grand Griffon Vendéen (still classified as a *limier* in modern French), modern English Otterhounds display the same leggy build (up to 27 inches high at the withers) as the otter hounds depicted in *Miroir de Phébus*. Moreover, Otterhounds work by much the same method as Gaston's otter hounds. As noted above, the otter den (or "holt" or "couch") resembles the beaver den in being hidden inside a watercourse bank with an underwater entrance. The otter couch differs from the beaver den in having a air vent in the bank above the den. An otter that is alarmed on land by the approach of a scentpack of Otterhounds on its drag slides down this vent into its burrow and escapes out the submerged entrance into the open water. Marking the underwater passage of the otter from the turbidity and bubbles in the water, the pack gives sight-chase along the bank and then dashes into the water, either to close immediately or to swim after the wash. Nothing in Gaston's text or illustration suggests that medieval otter-dogs were called upon to go to earth any more than modern Otterhounds are.

It is therefore impossible to argue by analogy of function for a similarity in appearance between the *Bibarhunt* and the medieval otter-dog. To constrain the appearance of the *Bibarhunt* by functional analogy, we need definite evidence of the appearance of medieval earth-dogs. Has any such evidence survived?

An illustration in the first English treatise on hunting—*Maystre of the Game*, compiled by Edward, Duke of York (1373-1415), comprised largely of translations from *Miroir de Phébus*—depicts three men and a long-legged hound at work during the unearthing of a hare (commonly misidentified as a fox). Before we rush to the conclusion that this image proves that medieval earth-dogs were long-legged, we must exercise due caution in interpreting the action. The hare, having been routed from its hole by two men digging into it, is pursued on the ground by a long-legged hound. Although its quarry is

indeed freshly unearthed, this hound is probably not an earth-dog at all but a *harrier* (a swift scenthound used both to trail and course hares) that has been held in check by the third man until the hare bolted its violated hole. As a matter of fact, the extant evidence suggests that the only animal entered by medieval hunters into hare holes was the trained ferret.

Has no unambiguous image of a medieval earth-dog come down to us? One such image has indeed been preserved in the very manuscript of *Miroir de Phébus* illuminated by the atelier of the Bedford Master that we have been examining and—*mirabile dictu*—it is the image of a badger-dog! Of the badger itself, Gaston Phébus writes:

Chapter XII. Of the badger and its habits.

The badger or grey is a fairly common animal; so it is unnecessary to describe it, for there are few people who have not seen on. Besides, I scarcely deign to speak of it, for it is not an animal that requires great skill to hunt nor that is hunted by dint of strength; for it neither flees nor sets off again in flight for very long; for the hounds pick up its scent almost immediately and close upon it baying, and then one can kill it easily.

It lives underground, or if it it goes out it is never very far from its burrow. It subsists on all kinds of field rodents and carrion, and on all fruits like the fox, but it dare not venture forth in the daytime: for it neither knows how nor is able to run away from danger. It spends its life sleeping more than anything else. They throw litters once a year, like foxes, and do so in their dens. When pursued, they defend themselves stoutly, and have a poisonous bite like foxes, but defend themselves even more stoutly than foxes. It accumulates more internal fat than any other animal in the world, on account of its sleeping so much, and its lard carries curative properties like that of the fox.

[*Chapitre XII. Du Blariau et de toute sa nature.*

Blariau ou taisson est assez commune beste; aussi n'ya-t-il pas lieu de le décrire, car il'y a peu de gens qui n'en aient vu. De plus, je n'entends gueres à parler de lui, car ce n'est pas une beste qu'il y ait maistrise à chasaer ni

qu'on chasse par force; car il ne fuit ou ne refuit gueres longuement; car les Chiens le tiennent tantost, où il se fait abbayer, et puis on le tuer voulentiers.

Demeure dedanz terre, ou s'il est hors il n'est gueres loing de taisnieres. Il vit de toutes vermines et charognes, et de toutes fruits comme le Regnard, mais il n'ose tant s'anuenturer le iour comme il fait: car il ne sçait ny ne peut fuir; il vit plus de dormir que d'autre chose; ils font vne fois l'an cheaux comme Regnards, et les font dedanz les fossez. Quant on les chasse ils se defendent fort, et ont leur morsure venimeuse comme Regnards, encores se defendent ils plus fort que le Regnard. C'est la beste du monde qui plus acueille de gresse dedanz, et pour long dormir qu'il fait, et son sain porte medecine comme celuy dy Regnard.]

The illuminated miniature accompanying the above passage shows ten badgers busy foraging and popping in and out of four burrow entrances. This is a verisimilitudinous pictorial conceit, inasmuch as the Eurasian badger (*Meles meles*) is in fact typically gregarious, living in "clans" of as many as twelve individuals who share digs in a "sett"—a labyrinthine "badger city" with as many as ten entrances. The text is factually correct, too, in its several statements that the badger never strays far from its den (the home range of a badger is in fact under four hundred yards); that a large portion of its nocturnally foraged diet consists of field rodents (the badger slashes open the burrows of field mice and voles with its long sharp foreclaws) and windfall fruit in autumn; that hounds can pick up its scent almost immediately (for the badger emits a fetid odor from its anal glands; the male emits an even ranker stench from its abdominal glands; whence the venerable French epithet that one is "stinking like a badger"); and, finally, the statement that the badger defends itself stoutly (for the Eurasian badger is in truth an ugly opponent who can master any individual dog his own size; his tough hide and elastic dermis, moreover, serve him well against the jaws of hounds; when fighting, the badger hisses, growls, snarls, and squeals—or, in the hunting

terminology approved by Turberville, he "shriketh").

Of the hunting of the badger, Gaston Phébus writes:

Chapter LVII. How to hunt and take badger.

And when the hunter wishes to hunt badger, he should seek out the earths and burrows where badger live; and, when the moon is clear, after midnight, he should stretch purse-nets over the mouths of the burrows. Then, in the morning, he should come with all his dogs to beat the bushes and rough country in the neighborhood of the sett and, as soon as they take fright of the dogs, the badgers will hasten to seek refuge in their earths and will be caught in the purse-nets; and if the dogs reach them beforehand, one will have good hunting and good sport: for they will close and bay as though it were a wild boar.

[Chapitre LVII. Comment on doit chasaer et prendre le blariau.

Et quant le veneur vouldra chasaer le tesson, il doit querir les terriers et tasnieres ou il demeure: et doit quant la lune sera clair, apres la mienuit tendre aux bouches des tasnieres les pouches. Puis le matin il doit venir a tout les chiens querir les hayes et fort pays environ les tasnieres et, des qu'ilz oiront l'effroy des chiens, ils se cuideront bouter dedanz les terriers, et seront prins es pouches, et si chiens les attaignent entre deux, on en aura bonne chasse et bon deduict: car ils se font abbayer comme vn sanglier.]

In the foreground of the single illuminated miniature accompanying this last little chapter are crowded each of the successive stages of the badger hunt that are described in the text—but herein represented as though happening simultaneously. From left to right, three tableaux are figured. In the first, a *valet de chiens* walking a couple of greyhounds on leash beats the undergrowth. In the second, two greyhounds, encouraged by *valets de chasse* armed with pike and mattock, tear to pieces a badger that they have caught outside its earth. In the third, a purse-net is shown stretched across a mouth of the badger's burrow.

Just as in our analysis of the painting of the otter hunt, we must impose the narrative order of the text on these three tableau-elements of the painting of the badger hunt. First, during the night, a purse-net is set across an entrance to its burrow while the badger is foraging outside; then, at dawn, the main hunting party of dogs and men arrives and beats the country about the sett; finally, the badger makes a short-legged break for his burrow but is run down and set upon in the open by the slipped greyhounds.

Upon closer inspection, the full subject treated in the miniature of the badger-hunt proves a bit trickier to analyze than that of the otter-hunt. For there are two vignettes conspicuously figured in the background of the Master of Bedford's painting of the badger-hunt that do not fit into the sequence of three tableaux just examined; nor do they correspond to any activity mentioned in the text. In one, an earth-stopper servant plugs another mouth of the sett with a big flaming ball compounded of criss-crossed twigs, leaves, and sulfurous rags. In the other background tableau, a third entrance to the sett is being entered by a dog whose nether half is yet visible; whilst two hunt servants are in the act of swinging down their mattocks to break into the badger earth.

Independently of the text that he is illustrating, the illuminator has taken the liberty of inserting these two latter tableaux in order to represent alternative methods of badger-hunting that are not mentioned by Gaston Phébus. Accordingly, the badger-hunt miniature in *Miroir de Phébus* requires even more complex interpretation than the otter-hunt miniature. The latter miniature represents diachronous events in one method of otter-hunting as though they were happening simultaneously (yet omits any representation of the alternative net-method described in the text). The former miniature represents three alternative methods of badger-hunting as though they were being used simultaneously (two of which methods are not even mentioned in the text).

As we have already seen, the three tableaux in the

foreground of the painting—the purse-net over the burrow entrance; the leash-hounds in the thicket; and the hounds biting the badger in the open—represent successive steps in the method of hunting to be employed in the event that the badger has come out of its earth to forage. By contrast, each of the two tableaux in the background of the painting represents a different method that may be used if the badger keeps to its earth.

The fourth tableau—the fumigation of the burrow—represents a method for bolting the badger from its den, whether into a purse-net or into the midst of a mob of packhounds. The fifth tableau—the dog being entered into the badger earth while the hunt servants dig above the noise of the underground fray—represents a method for bolting, baying, or drawing the badger.

Neither of these last two methods is mentioned in the text of Gaston Phébus. Indeed, the last method—putting earthdogs to earth to bolt, bay, or draw the badger—would not finally be reduced to literary exposition until the writings of Du Fouilloux (*ibid.*) a century-and-a-half later. Why should the artist of the badger-hunt miniature have elected in his background tableaux to supererogate the method recommended by Gaston Phébus in the text? Why did he take the liberty of representing methods that are not even obliquely alluded to in the text that he was ostensibly illustrating?

This discrepancy between text and picture might reflect a regional contrast in the badger-hunting techniques that were familiar to the author on one hand and to the artist and his patron on the other. Gaston Phébus hunted

in the extreme south of France. By contrast, the atelier of the Bedford Master was Parisian. The Master's eponymous English patron, the Duke of Bedford (1389-1435), campaigned extensively in France with his brother Henry V before assuming the French regency (1423-1435) for the infant Henry VI. It is not unreasonable to infer that, although badger-hunting with earth-dogs was contrary to the late medieval custom of southern France, it may have been the conventional practice in the great swathe of northern France then under English (properly, Anglo-Norman) suzerainty—Artois, Picardy, Normandy, Brittany, Champagne, and Burgundy. The attribution by Du Fouilloux (*ibid.*) of the origin of the *basset* to Artois and Normandy lends support to the notion that the practice of badger-hunting with earth-dogs originated in the northwest France.

Now, the sixty-four-thousand-dollar question: What does the earth-dog in the Bedford Master's miniature of the badger-hunt look like? Certainly, it is no greyhound. The whitish coat of this badger-seeking earth-dog is self-colored and wiry; its short-coupled loins are not tucked up; its hindlegs are not so long and fine as those of the greyhounds in the picture.

Nevertheless, the legs of the Bedford Master's earth-dog are of perfectly normal length and straightness. In fact, the nether half of this earth-dog is almost identical in appearance to the nether half of the dog sticking out of the hollow tree in the painting of the otter-hunt; which, in turn, is identical to that of the hound scent-trailing on the bank. There is no reason to expect that the invisible front half of the earth-dog in the painting of the badger-hunt should not look very like the front half of the hounds in the painting of the otter hunt—namely, *limiers*.

So here we have an exemplary image of the medieval French earth-dog entering a badger burrow—and it is a long-legged *limier*. We may venture to infer that sometime between the illumination of Gaston Phébus' hunting treatise at the beginning of the fifteenth century and the publication of Du Fouilloux' hunting treatise in the middle of the sixteenth century, short-legged earth-dogs were developed in France. In head and trunk, the *bassets* depicted in Du Fouilloux (1560) appear essentially indistinguishable from the *limiers* depicted in the same work; they differ in being short-legged. It seems both historically plausible and conformationally consistent to hypothesize that the *basset* was developed during the specified late medieval/early modern time-window by artificial selection for spontaneous micromelic achondroplastic mutation within the existing *limier* bloodstock, in line with the intra-breed dwarfing process speculatively discussed in Chapter 3 of the present work.

Another inference may be lifted from the Bedford Master's badger-hunt painting without the benefit of any speculative leverage: the inference, namely, that earth-dogs need not be short-legged. This generality turns out to apply to modern no less than to medieval breeds—as our following consideration of the evolution in meaning of the word *terrier* will prove.

In contrast to the swift surface-pursuit function common to the medieval trailing and coursing dogs—such as the otter hound, the tumbler, the lyemmer, and the greyhound—the specialized function of the medieval earth-dog was to go to ground and invade the *earth* (the den or burrow) of the stationary quarry immured there. The term *terrier* (from French *chien terrier*, meaning "dog used to start badgers, etc., from their *terrier*"; where *terrier* means "the earth or burrow of a fox or badger"; from late Latin *terrarium*, "mound of earth, burrow") has been applied to earth-dogs in French since the mid-fourteenth century and in English since the mid-fifteenth century. As a dog that "hunts underground", the eighth-century *bibarhunt* qualifies as a particular type of *terrier*. (Paradoxically, a secondary meaning of *terrier* in eighteenth-century English was "beaver"—designating the occupant of a burrow rather than its invader. Hypothetically, then, *bibarhunt* could have been translated into eighteenth-century English as *terrier-terrier*.)

The term *terrier* figures prominently in the first systematic treatise on English dogs: *De Canibus Britannicis* (London: Gulielmum seresium, 1570) by Johannes Caius

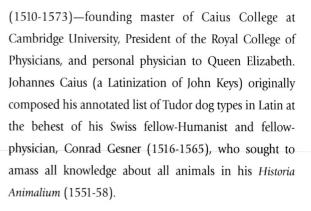

(1510-1573)—founding master of Caius College at Cambridge University, President of the Royal College of Physicians, and personal physician to Queen Elizabeth. Johannes Caius (a Latinization of John Keys) originally composed his annotated list of Tudor dog types in Latin at the behest of his Swiss fellow-Humanist and fellow-physician, Conrad Gesner (1516-1565), who sought to amass all knowledge about all animals in his *Historia Animalium* (1551-58).

Dr. Caius lists the Terrier (Latin *terrarius*; rendered variously into English as *Terrier, Terryer,* or *Terrar* in Abraham Fleming's translation of 1576, entitled *Of Englishe Dogges: the diversities, the names, the natures, and the properties*) as one of the seven breeds [namely: Harriers (*Leverarius*), Terriers (*Terrarius*), Bloodhounds (*Sanguinarius*), Gazehounds (*Agaseus*), Greyhounds (*Leporarius*), Lyemmers (*Lorarius*), and Tumblers (*Vertagus*)] subsumed within his general class of purebred hunting dogs (*Venatici generosi*). Under the heading of *Terrarius*, Caius writes:

> There are [scenthounds, *sagaces*] that hunt the fox and badger exclusively, whom we call Terriers: because they enter underground passages in the earth in the same manner as ferrets hunting rabbits; and there they terrorize and bite the fox and badger, in order either to tear it to pieces underground with their teeth, or else to drive it in flight out of the den into nets spread over the entrances of the tunnels. These are indeed the smallest in the class of scenthounds [the other two scenthound breeds listed by Caius being Harriers and Bloodhounds].

> *[Sunt, qui vulpem atque taxum solum, quos terrarios vocamus: quod subeant terrae cuniculos more viverrarum in Venatu cuniculorum, et ita terrent mordentque vulpem atque taxum, ut vel in terra morsu lacerent, vel e specu in fugam aut casses cuniculorum ostiis inductas compellant. Sed hi in sagacium genere minimi sunt.]*

Note that Dr. Caius supplies under his heading of

Terrier no physical description of the breed apart from mentioning that it is the smallest of the *Sagax* class. Under the heading of *Harrier*, however, Caius does supply a general physical description of his *Sagax* class—which includes the Terrier and the Bloodhound as well as the Harrier (Fleming's translation, *op. cit.*):

> Wee may knowe these kinds of Dogges [*Sagaces*] by their long, large, and bagging lippes, by their hanging eares, reachyng down both sydes of their chappes, and by the indifferent [medium-sized] and measurable [moderately-dimensioned] proportion of their making.

We may therefore infer of the physical appearance of the sixteenth-century British Terrier that it had pendulous lips and ears like the bloodhound—or, indeed, like the *bassets* pictured in Du Fouilloux (1560). Although Caius's description of the British Terrier as the "smallest of the "scenthounds" might

be construed to imply that it further resembled the contemporary French *basset* in being short-legged, Caius's word *minimi* is equally consistent with the Elizabethan Terrier having been just a proportionally smaller version of the other two long-legged scenthounds. If the Elizabethan Terrier were unusually short in the leg, it seems odd that Caius would have neglected to say as much to his medical colleague in Switzerland.

Nevertheless, the possibility that the "smallness" of Caius' British *Terrier* might have been the effect of short-leggedness receives a strong measure of support from three contemporary Elizabethan sources mentioned in the preceding chapter: two translations of Du Fouilloux (by Turberville in 1575 and by Surflet in 1600) and a play (by Shakespeare in 1594). The earliest of the three external sources supportive of the internal evidence in Caius' monograph of an identity between his *Terrarius* and Du Fouilloux' French *basset* is Turberville's translation of Du Fouilloux' pan-European bestseller, extensively cited in the preceding chapter. Throughout his translation of *La*

Vénerie into English, Turberville (1540-1610), translates French basset as English *terrier*.

Recall how Du Fouilloux' chapter (Ch. 60, *op. cit.*) on the subterranean hunting of fox and badger opens [present author's translation]:

> After having spoken of hunting with coursing dogs, I will undertake here a little treatise on hunting with **earth dogs**, and how one should train them to take fox, badger, and the like. It is first necessary to understand that we have two varieties of **Bassets**, concerning which we assert the original breed came from the regions of Flanders and Artois: of which the first variety have crooked legs and are generally short-haired: whereas the other variety have straight legs and predominantly coarse-haired, like water dogs.

Compare Turberville's translation (Chapter 65, *op. cit.*) of this passage:

> Now to speake of the **Foxhoundes and Terryers** and how you should enter them to take the Foxe, the Badgerd, and such like vermine: you muste understand that there are sundrie sortes of **Terriers**, whereof we hold opinion that one sorte came out of Flanders or the Lowe Countries, as Artoys and thereabouts and they have crooked legges, and are short heared most commonly. Another sorte there is which are shagged and streight legged.

Turberville's translation of Du Fouilloux, although in general not too bad, is fraught in this paragraph with glaring discrepancies. He translates *deux especes* as "sundrie sortes" rather than as precisely "two sorts". He attributes a Flemo-Artesian origin only to the crook-legged variety rather than to *la race* ("breed") that comprehends both the crook- and straight-legged varieties. Finally, Turberville translates *Bassetz* as "Terriers"; but he translates *Chiens de terre* as the duality "Foxhoundes and Terryers".

Turberville's different translations of these two French terms points up an opposition between French and English usage and practice in fossorial hunting with dogs. Du Fouilloux (*supra*) names but one physical type in the functional class *Chien de terre*: viz., the *Basset* (always short-legged; generally short-haired and crooked-legged; but sometimes rough-haired and straight-legged). Half-a-century later, as will be recalled from the preceding chapter, the French diplomat and lexicographer, Jean Nicot (1530-1600), stated in his entry under *"Basset"* in *Thresor de la Langue Françoyse* (1606) that the *"Basset*. Is a breed of earth dog...also called *chien terriers*, because they go to earth in the underground burrows and dens of badgers and foxes."

In writing that *bassets* "are also called *chiens terriers*," Nicot conforms to Du Fouilloux' usage in equating the words *Chien terrier* and *Basset*. By contrast, it may be inferred from Turberville's translation of *Chiens de terre* as "Foxhoundes and Terryers" that the English recognized two quite distinct physical types of earth-dog: viz., the long-legged, prick-eared foxhound and the short-legged, pendent-eared terrier. That Turberville's *terrier* corresponds in physical form as well as function to Du Fouilloux' Flemo-Artesian *basset* is supported by Turberville's invariable practice (some thirty more times, in fact) of translating *basset* as "terrier".

Richard Surflet (*op. cit.*) reinforces the likelihood that physical identity obtains between Du Fouilloux' *basset* in France and Turberville's "terrier" in England, for he casually imports Du Fouilloux' *basset* directly into his English translation without change. Recall the discussion in the preceding chapter of the woodcut in Du Fouilloux (*op. cit.*) that depicts the seigneur encouraging his young *bassets* to go to badger ground, crying to them, *"Coule à luy Basset, Coule à luy, hou, prenez prenez"* ["Crawl down to him, basset! Crawl down to him! Hoa! Sic'em! Sic'em!"]. Turberville, as is his wont, translates *Bassets* as "Terryers" in the pertinent passage from *La Vénerie:*

> Take out then all your old **Terryers**, and couple them up: then put in your yong **Terryers** and encourage them crying, "To him, To him, To him."

Compare Surflet's translation twenty-five years later

> Couple up all the old **earth dogs**, and after let loose the young ones, incouraging them to take the earth, and crying unto them, "Creepe into them **basset**, creep into them."

This first attested appearance of the word *basset* in English literature is consistent with the interpretation that the short-legged Elizabethan earth-dogs called "terriers" by Turberville were in fact Flemo-Artesian bassets. Finally, the proposition that French *bassets à jambes torses* were indeed present in Elizabethan England (at least on aristocratic estates) is ringingly matched by the pen of the Bard himself, who was a keen sportsman in the Warwickshire countryside.

In the Fourth Act of *A Midsummer Night's Dream* (1594), Shakespeare has Duke Theseus (who was, like the great Spartan hunter Castor, a student of the centaur Chiron) enumerate to Hippolyta the points of his dogs that prove that they are of the "Spartan" (known in Classical literature as the "Laconian" or "Castorian") breed of hounds:

> My hounds are bred out of the Spartan kind [breed],
> So **flew'd** [having pendulous chaps], so sanded [of sandy color]; and their heads are hung
> With **ears that sweep** away the morning dew;
> **Crook-kneed**, and **dew-lapp'd** like Thessalian bulls;
> **Slow** in pursuit, but matched in mouth like bells,
> Each under each [matched in their voices like a set of harmoniously pitched bells].   A cry more tuneable
> Was never holla'd to nor cheered with horn
> In Crete, in Sparta, nor in Thessaly.

Shakespeare describes the heads of his "Spartan hounds" in terms almost identical to those in which Caius describes the heads of his British "Terriers"—referring to their baggy lips ("flew'd" and "dew-lapp'd") and hanging ears ("their heads are hung with ears that sweep away the

little room for doubt that Shakespeare's "Spartan hounds" are transparent surrogates for sixteenth-century French *bassets à jambes torses*.

We have concluded our case for the argument that the Elizabethan "Terriers" described by Caius (1570) and Turberville (1575) are Continental imports indistinguishable in form from the sixteenth-century French Bassets described by Du Fouilloux (1560).

On the evidence extensively cited in the preceding chapter, a cogent case has been be made that the Austrian Baroque *Dachshund* was essentially indistinguishable in form as well as function from the sixteenth-century Flemo-Artesian Basset. Given our preceding argument that the Elizabethan "Terrier" was also essentially indistinguishable from the Flemo-Artesian Basset, then it follows that the Elizabethan "Terrier" and the early Dachshund were essentially indistinguishable from each other in form.

Our assertion that the Elizabethan "terrier" was really a French-style *basset* strikes the nose as outlandish on account of an historical discontinuity. From just after the end of Elizabeth's reign until the middle of Victoria's reign, the Continental-style *basset* goes missing in the British Isles. The imported *basset* appears to have gone to English ground during the reign of James I and mysteriously died there. The French basset was not formally reintroduced to Britain until the importation by Lord Galway of a pair of Le Couteulx hounds in 1866. Yet there appears to be a better than sporting chance that the *basset*-qua-*dachshund* may have been informally smuggled into Scotland from

the Continent in the latter part of the eighteenth century and folded into the native Caledonian terrier strains, as shall be argued below.

Before we consider the clues that hint so

qua-*terrier* seems to have been quite supplanted in the British sporting literature by a new class of *terrier* that was defined strictly by function without regard to physical type. In post-Elizabethan times, any dog that could be induced to go to earth and offer fight would qualify as a "Terrier", no matter how non-descript its appearance or accidental its parentage. In Stuart times, the *basset*-like physical elements that the Elizabethan writers had imputed to the English word *terrier* cease being remarked upon. Instead, working ability and suitable temperament become the only criteria for categorization as *terrier*.

Judging from the account given by Captain Jocelyn Lucas in his *Hunt and Working Terriers* (1931), the last extant instance of Elizabethan usage before this fundamental shift toward pure functionality in the meaning of the English word *terrier* comes from the pen of James I (1566-1625), that most literary of English kings. During the contentious years of his minority as James VI of Scotland, James was kept for safety in Stirling Castle under the protection of his guardian and regent, the 6th Earl of Mar. There he was educated by George Buchanan alongside the Earl's son, Sir John Erskine (1562-1634)—to whom James ever afterward applied his schoolboy sobriquet, "Jocky o' Sclaittes". Jocky succeeded as the 7th Earl of Mar in 1572, and went on to become James' most trusted favorite: guardian to James' son, Prince Henry; James' envoy to London in 1601 to confirm his succession to the English throne; member of the English Privy Council upon James' accession; Lord High Treasurer of Scotland; and James' private liaison with other European monarchs.

In 1605, Henry IV of France wrote the Earl of Mar desiring his good offices in securing the friendship of James I. Not unmindful that the "jewell of diamonds" accompanying Henry's letter was valued at 15,000 livres, the Earl of Mar did undertake to cultivate James' amity toward Henry. Now, James—though so spindly in the legs that he had to be strapped to his horse—was a bold rider and keen hunter. It need not therefore surprise us if King James would fain prove with one gesture his friendship toward the King of France and the superiority of Scottish hunting productions.

Sure enough, Captain Lucas informs us that James I wrote a letter to the Earl of Mar (deposited in the Menteith Charter) asking him to obtain three dogs from the Earl of Menteith (whose castle stood on a tiny island in the Lake of Menteith, twenty miles inland of Stirling Castle, in the picturesque region of southern Perthshire in which Sir Walter Scott would set *The Lady of the Lake* and *Rob Roy*) and send them (each in a separate ship for safety's sake) as a royal gift to the King of France. The dogs that James wants sent to his French counterpart are (as cited by Captain Lucas)

> some of those dogges they call **terrieres**, and in Scotlande **earthe dogges**, which are bothe stoute, good **for** killers, and will stay **longer** in the grounde.

Particular notice should be taken here of the comparative form of the final attributive that James I attaches to the Scottish earth-dogs: "will stay **longer** in the grounde." Longer than what? Longer than French terriers, of course; and—by extension— longer than the English *terrier*s bred from imported French *terrier*s. James' letter would seem to constitute the last instance in which the English word "terrier" is confined to the French-style *basset*. Unfortunately for this ingenious interpretation, however, it appears that Captain Lucas received a curiously corrupt version of the royal letter's text from his informant, Miss E.M. Debenham.

The full text of this letter, whose original, dated 17th August, 1617, is actually deposited in the

Mar and Kellie Charter (not the Menteith Charter), properly runs as follows (as cited by Andrew Hutchison in *The Lake of Menteith*, 1899):

> These are moste earnestlie to require you, as yee will do us most acceptable service and procure our exceeding greate contentment to searche oute and sende unto us two couple of excellent **terrieres or earth dogges**, which are both stout and good **fox** killers, and will stay **long** in the grounde. Wee are crediblie enformed that the Earle of Menteith hath good of that kinde, who wee are sure wilbe glade to gratifie us with them.

Handsome young William, the seventh Earl of Menteith (1588-1661), was of course only too glad to gratify the King. He went on to become a royal favorite and, during the interval 1628-1633, the most powerful official in Scotland. Observe what the King's letter in fact reveals about the earth-dogs that the Earl bred in his kennels on Inchcuan ("Dog Island") in the Lake of Menteith. They are equivalently called "terrieres"—not distinguished from them. They are "good fox killers"—not "good for killers." And they will stay "long in the grounde"—not "longer." In truth, James' letter provides no clue at all as to the appearance of these Scottish earth dogs *vis-à-vis* the French-style bassets across the border in England.

Rather than containing the last reference to the Elizabethan Basset *qua* "Terrier", James' letter is seen to contain the first instance of a new synonymy. Henceforth in British sporting literature, "terrier" serves as a simple synonym for "earth dog" in a purely functional sense of a "good killer that will stay long underground." No longer will "terrier" specifically connote "French style basset." Indeed, no post-Elizabethan allusions to the presence of a *basset*-like earth dog in England can be found at all before the middle of the nineteenth century (although see below Cox' remark regarding "the Scotish Sluth-hund").

The strictly functional definition of *terrier* as "earth dog"

remained the received usage for the next three centuries. A century after the publication of *De Canibus Britannicis*, for example, Richard Blome informed the readers of his *The Gentleman's Recreation* (1686) that a "terrier" could be got by crossing a beagle and a mongrel mastiff. Such a "terrier" was clearly no specimen of determinate physical type but simply any such mongrel as happened to prove itself useful at going to earth.

In 1737, Blome's terrier recipe was regurgitated by an anonymous poet who might from the quality of his blank verse be suspected of having fallen on his head in the world's oldest fox hunt, the Old Charlton in Sussex (*Records of the Old Charlton Hunt*, ed. Earl of March):

> Let Terriers small be bred, and taught to bay,
> When Foxes find unstopt Badjers earthe,
> To guide the Delvers, where to sink the Trench;
> ...Choose a fighting Curr, who lyes
> And scarce is heard, but often kills the Foxe;
> With such a one, bid him a Beagle join,
> The smallest kind, my Nymphs for Hare do use.
> That Cross gives Nose, and wisdom to come in
> When Foxes earth, and houndes all bayeing stand.

Later still, in 1802, William B. Daniel in his *Rural Sports* uncritically repeated Blome's advice about getting good terriers by crossing beagles and mongrel mastiffs. Advocacy of a strictly functional connotation for "Terrier" continued right into the twentieth century. James Watson in *The Dog Book* (1906) demurred at the new British convention (eventually adopted by the AKC in 1931) of classifying the Dachshund as a member of the Hound Group on morphological grounds. (By contrast, the FCI divides the various breeds included in the AKC Hounds Group into three separate Groups: Scenthounds, Sighthounds, and Dachshunds.) Watson argued that the Dachshund rightly belonged in the Terrier Group, in accordance with the functional criterion that it had been developed as an earth-dog.

But Watson was backing a quixotic cause. With the establishment of national dog breed clubs in the last quarter of the nineteenth century, the functional definitions of the traditional working-dog types had begun to fray rapidly. Dog breed clubs installed a whole new regulatory machinery of written standards, competitive shows, and official studbooks. This machinery both permitted and promoted the genetic retooling of generalized working-dog types into arbitrarily precise new breeds. From the continuum of physical traits tolerated within a functionally-defined working-dog type, each emergent breed club selected one very precise subset of traits to fix as the hallmark of its proprietary breed. All the other permutations of traits that had formerly been acceptable in the working-dog type were now slated for systematic elimination from the club breedstock.

The intense new selective pressures brought to bear by the breed clubs tended to whittle each regional working-dog type into several distinct breeds, each reproductively isolated from its cousin breeds. The fate of the traditional short-legged terriers of Scotland provides an instructive example of this fissile tendency in the burgeoning dog fancy of the late nineteenth century that is particularly relevant to parallel developments in the Dachshund group in Germany.

A comparison of the historical processes of breed diversification and formalization in Scottish terriers (this latter term to be taken in the generic sense that embraces the precursors of all the modern short-legged terrier breeds of Scotland: namely, of the Scottish, Skye, West Highland White, Cairn, and Dandie Dinmont Terriers) and in Dachshunds is all the more apposite in view of three broad similarities between the two types. Functionally, both Scottish terriers and Dachshunds were developed as earth-dogs. Morphologically, both were framed to be short-legged and long-bodied. Genetically, the two types have exchanged blood.

Breed historians have traced genetic flow

between Dachshunds and Scottish terriers in both directions. In one direction, the short-legged Scottish terriers are definitely known to have entered the seminal blood lines of certain modern Dachshund breeds (see below). In the opposite direction, Dachshund blood has been credited on morphological grounds by the most eminent terrier auth-orities of both the twentieth century (John T. Marvin and A. Croxton Smith) and the nineteenth century (D.J. Thom-son Gray and Stone-henge) with having contributed essen-

tially to the early development of short-legged Scottish terriers.

In support of their morphological judgment, these same authorities have adduced historical channels permissive of the transmission of Continental dachshund stock into Scotland. We now return, as promised above, to the proposition whether "the *basset*-qua-*dachshund* may have been informally smuggled into Scotland from the Continent in the latter part of the eighteenth century and folded into the native Caledonian terrier strains."

The necessary first step in assessing this proposition—an examination of the early records bearing on the varieties of Scottish dogs—yields a striking chronological datum to conjure with. Although Scottish *terriers* in the functional sense are first described in the sixteenth century, the first evidence of disproportionate short-leggedness in a Scottish terrier dates only to the nineteenth century.

Consider the sixteenth-century Scottish record. In *De origine, moribus et rebus gestis Scotorum* ("Of the origin, customs and history of the Scots") (1578), John Leslie (1527-1596)—Bishop of Ross and intimate advisor to Mary Queen of Scots, for whose private edification he wrote the above treatise—writes (as translated into Scots by Father James Dalrymple in 1596 under the title, *The Historie of Scotland*):

Mairover because we heir have maid mentione of the hunting, sumthing in lyk manner we will say of the

dogs...Is it another **kynde of slwthhundes laich of stature bot braid of body**, because thar invadeng the cunings under the earth, throuch violence out of thair Lairis and Dennis he dryues the foxi, the matrix, the brok and the wilkatt: This kynde gif at ony time he fynd the passage narrow, that he can nocht entir undir the eard, he with his feit makes it large and apnes it vpe, and that with sik trauail, that oft tymes he is lost throuch his Diligence.

[Having described the various forms of hunting in Scotland, we will describe the corresponding varieties of hunting dogs...There is another **breed of sleuth-hound low of stature but broad of body**, befitting their invading the rabbits under the earth; through violence he drives out of their lairs and dens the fox, the marten, the badger, and the wildcat. This kind, if at any time he find the passage so narrow that he cannot enter under the earth, enlarges it with his feet and opens it up, and does so with so much exertion, that often he is lost through his diligence.]

The sleuth-hound is an historic Scottish type of the bloodhound—attested as early as the fourteenth century but extinct since the end of the eighteenth century. Note that neither Leslie nor his 16th-century translator actually supplies a specific name for the "kynde of slwthhundes" described here; nor do they supply names for any of the other varieties of hunting dogs that they describe. Note also that Leslie supplies no physical description of this earth-entering variety of Scottish sleuth-hound beyond his characterisation of it as "laich of stature bot braid of body."

An earlier Scottish historian, however, does offer a description of the coat-color of Scottish sleuth-hounds in general. Hector Boece (*c.* 1465 - *c.* 1536) writes in his *Scotorum Historiae* (1527; translated into Scots by John Bellenden as *The Hystory and Croniclis of Scotland*, 1536):

[There] ar thre maner of doggis in Scotland, quhilk ar sene in na vthir partis of the warld...The thrid kynd is mair than any rache, reid hewit or ellis blak with small spraingis of spottis, and ar callit be the peple **sleuthoundis**...He that denyis entres to the sleuthound...sal be haldin participant with the crime and thift committit.

[There are three varieties of dogs in Scotland that are seen in no other parts of the world...The third variety, called by the [Scots] people "sleuth-hounds", is more red-colored or else black with small streaks of spots than any [other] scenthound... Whoever refuses right-of-way to the sleuth-hound...shall be held accessory to the crime and theft committed.]

Boece's description of the Scottish sleuth-hound's coat color and tracking ability is consistent with a later identification of the Scottish sleuth-hound with the European bloodhound (the pendulous-eared and -flewed *Brache* or *braque*) propounded by Nicholas Cox (*The Gentleman's Recreation*, 1674): "The **Blood-hound** differeth nothing in quality from the Scotish **Sluth-hound**."

Taking into account Cox's physical identification of the Scottish sleuth-hound with the European blood-hound (which was in turn identified with the French *limier*) together with Leslie's characterization of his earth-entering variety of the Scottish sleuth-hound as "laich of stature", Leslie's sixteenth-century Scottish earth dog clearly bore a far nearer resemblance to the French *basset* than to any of our modern Scottish terriers. Furthermore, just as we have observed already with respect to Caius' description of his *terrarius*, Leslie's description does not necessarily imply  that his Scottish earth dog breed had disproportionately short legs. The modern Border Terrier, for instance, is only ten inches high and decently "braid of body"—yet has legs of proportionately normal length.

The first putative literary evidence of short-leggedness in the British terrier is not found until 1790, when Thomas Bewick and Ralph Beilby, printing partners of Newcastle, describe in *A General History of Quadrupeds* the "rough Terrier" (as opposed to the "smooth Terrier"):

There are two kinds of Terriers,—the one rough, short-legged, long-backed, very strong, and most commonly of a black or yellowish colour, mixed with white.

Bewick's accompanying wood engraving of the rough Terrier reveals, however, a dog that is very much longer-legged than our modern Scottish terriers. As a matter of fact, the first definite evidence of a disproportionately short-legged British terrier is not found until 1800, as one of five types of the Terrier represented in a plate in Sydenham Edwards' *Cynographia Britannica*. Edward's text refers to a terrier race peculiar to Scotland, but without correlating it to the types depicted in the plate and without mentioning short-leggedness:

In Scotland, the use of the Terrier is to kill; and here they breed a fierce race. Great is their courage, they will attack and destroy the largest foxes with which the country abounds, following them into chasms of rocks, where they often perish together.

In fact, the first unambiguous evidence of a disproportionately short-legged Scottish terrier is not found until 1829, when Thomas Brown carefully describes (in *Biographical Sketches and Authentic Anecdotes of Dogs*) "three distinct varieties of the Scotch terrier," two of which are disproportionately short-legged. If disproportionately short-legged varieties of Scottish *terrier*s were not developed until the eigh-teenth or even nineteenth century, the question natur-ally arises whether such development might not have depended on crossbreeding with dachshunds or bassets imported from the Continent. To this question, John Marvin—dean of modern Scottish terrier writers—advances the following answer in *The New Complete Cairn Terrier* (1975):

Jacques Fouilloux, *La Venerie*, circa 1560, includes a woodcut showing men and dogs digging out badger...Undoubtedly, these early ground-going hounds were crossed with dogs of Terrier blood, which offers an explanation for many characteristics indigenous [*sic*] to various Terrier strains. Croxton Smith, in his chapter on Basset Hounds found in Drury's *British Dogs*, 3rd ed., 1903,...brings the small Basset (*a jambes torses*) into close relationship with the Dachshund Terrier. The only explanation of the infusion of the Basset or Dachshund blood into the Terrier breeds is the invasion of the French and German strains as companions of itinerant Gypsies who went back and forth between the British Isles and their homeland. These hypotheses are supported by Stonehenge and Gray in later works of authority.

Lest such a Gypsy-Scotland connection seem a wee bit far-fetched, it should be noted that Gypsies were indeed a presence to be reckoned with in Scotland from the beginning of the sixteenth century. In 1505, James IV of Scotland gave the "Count of Little Egypt" (a Gypsy chieftain) a letter of recommendation to the King of Denmark. In 1540, James V granted the "Earl of Little Egypt" exclusive authority to hang all "Egyptians" (as the Germans had christened the Manush tribe of itinerant Gypsies that appeared in Northern Europe in the fifteenth century) in his realm. Scotland's chronically troubled Highlands and Borders afforded a lawless haven for Manush groups expelled from the more ordered territories of France, Alsace, and Germany during periodic crack-downs on Gypsy vagrancy. Manush men enjoyed a particular reputation as traders in livestock of dubious ownership, circus performers, animal trainers, and dog handlers.

The special competence of the Manush with animals figures in Sir Walter Scott's second novel, *Guy Mannering* (1815), set in the southwest Scottish Border Country in the second half of the eighteenth century. Dandie Dinmont—the generous-hearted, hunting-obsessed farmer whose fictional name has been assigned to the real successors of the originals of his tribe of "Mustard and Pepper" terriers that he "regularly entered wi' the tods and brocks [foxes and badgers]"—hires a Gypsy

tod-hunter's "gang" headed by Tod Gabbie (a North Sea smuggler nick-named for his legal employment as a "fell [clever] fox-hunter") to assist the local sportsmen in a week given over to fox-, otter-, and badger-hunting.

> On this last occasion [badger-hunting], after young Pepper had lost a fore-foot and young Mustard the second had been nearly throttled, [Scott's young hero, Guy Mannering] begged...of Mr. Dinmont, that the poor badger, who had made so gallant a defence, should be allowed to retire to his earth without further molestation... "Weel," said [Mr. Dinmont], "that's queer aneugh! But since ye take his part, deil a tyke [dog] shall meddle wi' him mair in my day...but, Lord save us, to care about a brock!"

Smiling at his usual disingenuous disclaimers (Scott persisted in denying authorship of his own novels until 1827), those privy to the Abbotsford circle entertained not the slightest doubt that the Author of *Waverley* had drawn both the character and habits of Dandie Dinmont after those of his quaint real-life friend, James Davidson. To serve his passion for tod- and brock-hunting on his wild hill farm above Teviotdale, Davidson—as was universally credited—had developed the new breed of short-legged terrier celebrated in *Guy Mannering*.

This breed of his "ain fancy" Davidson called in its collectivity "Pepper and Mustard", in keeping with his conceit of surnaming every individual in it either "Mustard" or "Pepper" depending on coat color. Upon the publication of *Guy Mannering*, the race of "Pepper and Mustard" became an overnight sensation, coveted under the designer label of "Dandie Dinmont terrier" by novel-reading sportsmen throughout the British Isles. Scott himself so doted on a breeding brace of "Pepper and Mustard" given him by his rustic friend that Sir Edwin Landseer included a "Mustard" in his posthumous portrait of Scott with his dogs, entitled *The Rhymer's Glen*.

The author of *Guy Mannering* has the sportsmen in Dandie Dinmont's hunting party carry on lengthy parallel discussions of the merits of Davidson's badger-hunting terriers and of the merits of the hired Gypsy huntsmen. Why does Scott plait these two themes together so tightly? It was Scott's established practice to base many of the genre episodes in his Waverley novels on oral anecdotes related to him by country folk during his years in the field as a Borders ballad-collector. Is Scott perhaps hinting here at some private communication from Davidson linking the Gypsies to his "Pepper and Mustard" breed? Might some Gypsy original of Scott's Tab Gabbie character have supplied Davidson with a dachshund or basset that had been abducted in Germany or France and then spirited over the North Sea in a smugglers' lugger; which dwarf-legged foreign hound Davidson then crossed with local normal-legged Border terriers to launch his para-eponymous breed of dwarf-legged Scottish terriers?

Possibly. But it is also possible that Scott is obliquely alluding here to another oral tradition floating about the Borders. According to a statement by Archibald Steel, a prominent nineteenth-century breeder of Dandies in Kelso (cited in D.J. Thomson Gray, *The Dogs of Scotland: Their Varieties, History, Breeding, Exhibition, and Management*, 1887):

> It has been determined, with as much accuracy as possible in the circumstances, that a terrier closely resembling the modern Dandie Dinmont in form, character, and habits, and which was also used for similar purposes, was almost exclusively in the possession of the numerous families of tinkers and muggers who frequented the wild country on the southern slopes of the Cheviots...The first authentic record of the existence of this favorite terrier shows it to have been in the hands of the famous 'Piper Allan', who, when at home, resided in the village of Holystone...in the wildest portion of Upper Coquetdale [on the Northumbrian side of the Cheviot Hills, twenty miles east of Davidson's farm on Rule Water]. Allan is reputed to have kept in those days the largest kennel of eight or nine terriers, principally used in otter hunting...Mr Francis Somner, now the oldest living

breeder of Dandies [having dispersed his kennel in 1842], purchased 'Old Pepper' from a grandson of the old piper.

"Tinkers and muggers" (menders of metal utensils and peddlars of earthenware), is the Scottish colloquialism for "Gypsies". Just fifteen miles from both Piper Allan's Holystone and Dandie Dinmont's Rule Water lies the remote Cheviot Hills village of Kirk Yetholm—capital of the Borders Manush, home of the once great Romany family of Faa. Ten thousand Gypsies foregathered in Kirk Yetholm in 1898 for the coronation of Charles Faa Blyth, though his palace was but a two-room cottage. A vital connection is known to have existed between Piper Allan and the Gypsies.

In 1863, Robert White of Newcastle-on-Tyne recorded that Piper Allan was half-Gypsy himself (cited in Gray, *op. cit.*):

> The father of Jamie Allan (Piper Allan) was named William, and was born at Bellingham in 1704...In early life he became a good player on the bagpipes...He mended pots and pans, made spoons, baskets, and besoms, and was a keen and excellent fisher. In the valley of Coquet he married a gipsy girl named Betty, who bore him six children, and James [born in 1734] was the youngest save one. Among his other pursuits, he [William] excelled especially in the hunting of otters, and kept eight or ten dogs for that particular sport.

Perhaps Davidson derived his bloodstock from Piper Allan's line of terriers and Scott had such a pedigree in mind when he juxtaposed Gypsies with "Pepper and Mustard" in *Guy Mannering*. Whatever the route, a deal of circumstantial evidence prompts the idea that Gypsies may have channeled dachshunds or bassets to the first breeders of short-legged Scottish terriers.

Still, other scenarios may be entertained. Perhaps noble adherents of the Stuart cause who had joined the Pretenders in their French exile carried bassets back to

Scotland with them after the Act of Indemnity of 1747. Perhaps Scottish mercenary soldiers brought dachshunds back home with them after tours of duty in the German principalities. Perhaps some unsung Scottish breeder succeeded at fixing spontaneous achondroplastic mutation within the indigenous normal-legged terrier population. Or perhaps an indigenous turnspit component or some remnant of medieval Scottish earth-going sleuth-hound was folded into the terrier stock. Who knows? Ask Alice.

By contrast, we know the exact path of genetic flow from Scottish terriers into modern Dachshunds. In the first monograph ever written on the Dachshund breed (*Der Dachshund*, 1896), Major a.D. Emil Ilgner—co-founder with Count Claus Hahn of the *Deutscher Teckelklub* (DTK) in 1888—described the contemporary effort in Germany to reconstruct the extinct Wire-haired Dachshund that

was thought to have been produced in the previous century by crossing the Smooth-haired Dachshund with the "Wire-haired Pinscher" (precursor of the modern Schnauzer). Ilgner writes, referring to the late 1880s:

> At the time, buyers of horses from Mecklenburg came to England, and on their return to Germany took with them specimens of different *terrier* breeds, among them the Dandie Dinmont *terrier*s, which dogs possessed a perfect Dachshund conformation, and they were used for crossing with a Smooth-haired Dachshund. Without doubt, I consider this crossing more adequate than any other, as it created a perfect type more quickly...The preponderance of this small English [*sic*] breed is marked by the circumstance that even today one sees Wire-haired Dachshunds whose hair is too soft on the head.

(Of course, it need hardly surprise us that "Dandie Dinmont terriers... possessed a perfect Dachshund conformation" if James Davidson developed his Dandie Dinmont breed by crossing wire-haired Border terriers with imported dachshunds.) According to Lois Meistrell (*The New Dachshund*, 1976), German breeders of

Wire-haired Dachshunds subsequently folded Scottish Terrier, Skye Terrier, and Wire Fox Terrier into their lines in order to harden the Dinmont coat and suppress the Dinmont topnotch. The Scottish terrier breeds proved even more desirable to the German dog fancy in their unadulterated state. According to Leonard Naylor (*Dachshunds*, 1937), British terriers were much more numerous in Germany than Dachshunds in the decades leading up to the Second World War. (Indeed, Eva Braun out-Fala'd FDR by doting on a brace of black Scotties: Stasi and Negus, who both detested Blondi.)

In the 1920s, dissatisfaction in German hunting circles with the digging ability and attack instinct of the current Dachshund breeds chafed against a nationalistic reluctance to depend on otherwise satisfactory British terriers. As a result, a new national breed—the leggy, smooth-coated *Deutsche Jagdterrier* (German Hunt Terrier)—was developed for going to earth after badger and fox. Actually, this breed's name is a bit of a fudge. Although the cocktail was mixed in Germany, all the ingredients (Welsh Terrier plus Lakeland Terrier plus Fox Terrier) were British.

Only after the Second World War did the Dachshund breed attain a level of popularity in Germany on par with that which it enjoyed in America and Britain. The great popularity of the Dachshund in Britain—interrupted only by the First World War—dated all the way back to 1840, when Prince Albert brought his dachshunds along with him to when he married Queen Victoria. Indeed, the world's first dog show to feature a Dachshund entry was British (the Birmingham Dog Show, 1870); as was the world's first dog show to feature a Dachshund class (Crystal Palace, 1873); as was the world's first Dachshund club (the Dachshund Club, founded in 1881) and Dachshund standard (The Dachshund Standard, 1881).

Today, however, the world's avowedly biggest Dachshund club (IDG) and the global FCI Breed Standard (adopted by the DTK in 1925) are both German. The *Internationaler Dackel-Club Gergweis e.V.* (IDG) is headquartered in Osterhofen, a picturesque Bavarian town in the Danube valley fifty miles downriver of von Hohberg's seventeenth-century estate. Kathi Dorfmeister—foundress of the IDG and charismatic breed patroness whose international postal address was officially recognized as *Dorfmeister im Dackeldorf* ("Dorfmeister in Dachshund-Town")—died in 1998 at age 87. Dissenting from the DTK emphasis on hunting competence and aggressive disposition, Dorfmeister laid down the IDG counter-policy that modern Dachshunds should bred exclusively for genial companionship.

Under IDG auspices, the village of Gergweis in the suburbs of Osterhofen breeds Dachshunds that are intended solely to be pets. Although these Dachshunds are ineligible for DTK registration, they have proven so popular with the European public that Gergweis has become a tourist mecca. Plans are afoot to honor Dorfmeister's passing at the Whitsuntide Weltsiegerschau ("World Champion Show") in the year 2000 with a huge memorial service to be attended by thousands of "Dachshund-friends" and their respectfully barking Dachshunds.

Having thus touched on the vexed but fascinating question of the extent of the actual genetic overlap between Dachshunds and Scottish terriers, we now return to our review of the processes of breed formalization and working-dog denaturing as they were progressively applied to both Dachshunds and Scottish terriers beginning in the latter part of the nineteenth century.

The program of a London dog show in 1862 essayed a class distinction between *Skye Terriers* and *Scotch Terriers* based on contrasting coat characteristics. The proposed distinction was roundly ignored by Scottish terrier people. For the next twenty years, *Skye Terrier* and *Scotch Terrier* continued to be used *ad libitum* as synonymous omnibus terms embracing all those varieties of Scotch terrriers that Brown had carefully described as physical types back in 1829 but that were half-a-century later still not discriminated by name.

Scots disdained English attempts to assign formal names to the various physical types of the Scottish terriers for the perfectly good reason that (apart perhaps from the occasional private strain) they simply did not breed true. In contrast to, say, Scottish deerhounds, which were sedulously bred one to another in estate kennels in order to ensure their conformity to a Lord Dumbello ideal of physical perfection, Scottish terriers belonged to the proletariat of Scottish dogdom. As such, Scottish terrier puppies plopped in all shapes and colors off the messy palette of canine promiscuity. Terrier-types with demonstrated working ability were suffered to live and reproduce at will. Useless dogs were bucketed before they were competent to get up to reproductive mischief.

Not until breed clubs began to be organized under the aegis of the Kennel Club (founded in 1873) did the breeding of Scottish terriers to type begin as a systematic public enterprise. The Scottish terrier world rapidly aligned itself into several named domains: *Skye terrier* now connoted drop ears and long hair; *Scottish terrier* connoted prick ears and rather short hair; *Dandie Dinmont* connoted drop ears and soft-haired topnotch. Over the course of the next several decades, schisms amongst shifting coalitions of Scottish breeders successively abstracted from the traditional generalized prick-eared Highland Scotch terrier working stock three distinct new breeds, each defined and defended by its own breed club: the Scottish Terrier (whose first stable breed club was founded in 1882); the West Highland White Terrier (1904); and the Cairn Terrier (1912).

By the mid-nineteenth century in Germany, by contrast, taxonomists (e.g., Fitzinger, 1867: *supra*) had already discriminated ten sub-species of the Dachshund "species"—including Long-haired and Wire-haired Dachshunds. Yet, at the time of the founding of the DTK in 1888, only the Standard Smooth Dachshund was sufficiently fixed in its development to warrant description in the first German standard of points written in 1889 (or, for that matter, in the British standard of 1881). Long-haired and Wire-haired Dachshunds—although they had been dignified with their own Linnaean names in German taxonomies of the dog—were not then fixed into stable, homozygous breeds (and Miniature Dachshunds did not exist at all). Individual long-haired and wire-haired Dachshunds were inherently unstable types at the time of the founding of the national breed clubs for one of two reasons. Either they were heterozygous (whether as once-off products of individual outcrosses or as accidental throws of smooth parents); or they were products of small, private strains that would quickly succumb to genetic debilitation unless outcrossed.

As a result, the formation of breed clubs dedicated to the Longhaired, Wirehaired, and Miniature Dachshunds lagged well behind the original Dachshund clubs, which were implicitly dedicated to the Standard Smooth Dachshund. Although Longhaired and Wirehaired Dachshunds were shown informally in Germany in the 1880s, not until 1915 did the DTK studbook (opened in 1890) begin to discriminate the three coat types.

Although the three coat types were shown in separate classes in Germany after the First World War, it remained accepted practice until after the Second World War to cross both Long- and Wirehaired lineages to Smooth lineages as often as required to correct deviations from Dachshund type (especially with respect to shortness of leg and hardness of coat). In Britain and the United States as well, breeders of Longhaired and Wirehaired Dachsunds regularly crossed to Smooth lines for decades after their national Kennel Clubs authorized separate classifications for Longhaired and Wirehaired Dachshunds in the 1930-31. Until the practice of outcrossing was disallowed in all three countries after the Second World War, Dachshund litters thrown by registered parents of

the same coat type commonly contained other coat types as well.

Similarly, Miniature Dachshund lines in the first decades of the miniature breed's development had frequently to be crossed with counterpart Standard lines to preserve type and vigor. Germany had much the headstart over Britain and the United States in the development of Miniature Dachsunds. In Germany, the DTK recognized the *Kaninchenteckel* and *Zwerg* classes in 1912. In the United States, on the other hand, Miniature Dachshunds were not granted recognition by the DCA as a separate variety until 1951. Despite starting up their Miniature Dachshund programs at different times, all three countries condoned the practice of rectifying Miniature lines with Standard outcrosses into the 1960s.

The necessity of outcrossing arbitrarily demarcated breeds to their cousin breeds in order to preserve type was producing the same effect in the new Scottish terrier breeds as in the new Dachshund breeds. Continuing well into the twentieth century, single litters of Scottish Terriers commonly contained marketable specimens of all three recognized Scottish terrier breeds. Not until the 1920s did each of these three breed populations become large and genetically robust enough that their respective breed clubs could succeed at imposing such discipline on Terrier breeders as to ensure that all registered matings bred true.

The driving aims of any breed club are strong product differentiation and quality control. The forms of the modern breeds that were carved out of the traditional Scotch terrier became institutionally enshrined as ends in themselves. Form decoupled and drifted apart from the earth-dog function that was the sole end of the common ancestor. In the names "Scottish Terrier", "West Highland White Terrier", and "Cairn Terrier", the appellative "Terrier" has been largely drained of its erstwhile functional connotation and retained only as a nostalgic vestige of common ancestry.

As employed nowadays, the name "Terrier" has degenerated into an all-but-meaningless tag gratuitously conferred or withheld by registry authorities. Although nominally a functional class of earthdogs, the AKC Terrier Group includes amongst its twenty-five member breeds some that can pretend to only the most tenuous links with actual earthdogs. No less inconsistently, the AKC Terrier Group excludes various other breeds that either are practicing earthdogs or else were derived from such.

Of course, the AKC Terrier Group does include some breeds (such as the Fox Terriers) that have continuously and routinely been put to earth (and therefore continue to qualify as *terriers* in the practical sense). But it includes a greater number of breeds (such as the five Scottish terrier breeds) that—though their ancestry can be directly traced to traditional earth-dog stock—by and large ceased being put to earth a century or so since (and can therefore scarcely be treated as active *terrier* breeds in the functional sense).

As early as 1912, terrierist Arthur Blake Heinemann ("Hunt Terriers" in October issue of *The Foxhound*) was complaining noisily of dude terriers:

> Another time a lady brought down her team of white West Highland terriers, but they would not go to ground, find or bay a badger there, or join in a worry with a dead badger, and she said they didn't like the noise of the diggers shouting, and the noise of their spades and picks, nor the brambles at the mouth of the earth. A third time a youth brought some pretty Dandie-Dinmonts down, and told us yarns about their pluck. These next day would not go to ground, or look at a badger. Noise again!

Two decades later, the transformation of the Scottish terriers from working dogs to pets was complete. As Arthur Frederick Jones (pundit of the Scottie breed during its 1930s heyday when it was the third most popular breed in the United States) put it: "Hearth not hunt is the terrier's focus today."

At its most tenuous and conjectural extreme, the AKC Terrier Group includes several breeds (such as the American Staffordshire Terrier—less euphemistically known as the Pit Bull) that are styled "Terriers" only because it is speculatively supposed that they owe some remote ancestral fraction to earth-dog stock—even though they were themselves never intended to do a lick of earth-dog work and would be more appropriately dubbed pit "Terrors" than earth "Terriers".

Further muddling the clarity of the original usage of *terrier*, the AKC Terrier Group excludes some breeds (such as the Yorkshire Terrier and the Jack Russell Terrier) despite their both being labeled "Terriers" and actually descended from earth-dog stock. It also excludes certain breeds (such as the Tibetan Terrier) that are unaccountably called "Terriers" despite lacking any earth-dog ancestry or aptitude. Finally, as noted above, the AKC Terrier Group excludes the earthdog *par excellence*—the Dachshund, in all its manifold varieties. Go figure! (Actually, the Terrier Group is one of the few Groups to which the AKC has never assigned the Dachshund. Before ending up in the Hound Group in 1931, the Dachshund had been shuffled in and out of both the Working Group and the Sporting Group.)

Setting aside these objections, let us consider the twenty breeds in the AKC Terrier Group that are either practicing earthdogs or descended from traditional earth-dog stock. Forty percent of these twenty breeds are short-legged; sixty percent have legs of normal length. Significantly, all the AKC Terrier breeds that have found continuous regular employment in going to earth over the last century (such as the Border Terrier, Lakeland Terrier, and Fox Terrier) possess straight legs of normal length (as, of course, does the fox itself).

A concerted movement is afoot, of late, to restore some working luster to the short-legged terrier breeds in the United States. In 1971, Patricia Lent founded the American Working Terrier Association (AWTA) in Geneseo, New York, to promote the breeding and training of terriers possessed of the conformation and temperament requisite for them to go to earth as working dogs. In accordance with its functional program, the AWTA revived the traditional functional definition of *terrier*, such that it comprehends the

Dachshund in company with the working Terriers *soi-disant*.

The AWTA stages pass-fail artificial den trials in which any terrier belonging to one of nineteen designated pure breeds* can earn a Certificate of Gameness by executing the following routine: enter a 9-inch-square artificial tunnel; crawl the maze-like, game-scented length of the tunnel to a barred quarry box fitted with a trap door on top; and there "work" (bark, growl, dig, bite, and lunge at) a safely caged tame rat to the satisfaction of the judge. In addition, the AWTA awards Working Certificates to dogs of these same breeds who demonstrate the ability and gameness to enter a natural earth; work down to wild quarry (in the United States: red fox, badger, and woodchuck); and either bay, draw, or bolt it. In the United States, Standard Dachshunds are put to earth for fox and badger; Miniature Dachshunds are put to earth for woodchuck; and the smallest Minis (corresponding to the DTK/FCI *Kaninchen* class) are put to earth for rabbit.

In 1994, the AKC inaugurated its own program of non-competitive title-issuing Earthdog Tests, conceptually patterned on the AWTA artificial den trials but differing somewhat in respect of permissible breeds.** With 53 AKC-endorsed tests held nationwide in 1997, the AKC Earthdog Trials have stolen the thunder from the AWTA Den Trials, so that the AWTA has redirected its primary mission to the promotion of mortal field hunting.

Although programs promoting the refurbishment of the working potential of terriers in the United States have grown at an impressive rate since their inception in 1971, it would be unwarranted to infer that a significant proportion of the U.S. terrier population (including Dachshunds) has been recruited to underground service. Stepping from 1995

to 1996, for example, annual entries in AKC Earthdog Tests increased by a whopping 37 per cent. Nevertheless, the total number of such entries (including multiple entries by the same individual) in 1996 was only 3,218—thus representing less than 0.3 % of the aggregate of living AKC-registered individuals of the 21 eligible breeds. Statistically, A.F. Jones' old dictum about the modern terrier's focus being "hearth not hunt" still applies to the United States in spades.

In Europe, the situation is quite different. In Germany, where the world's first organized den trials were held at the end of the nineteenth century (although the use of artificial earths in training earth dogs had already been a practiced in Europe for at least three centuries: see *supra* Du Fouilloux, Ch. 60), the employment of Dachshunds and Terriers in both simulated earth work and genuine hunting of the full gamut of fossorial quarry has been continuous and widespread throughout the last century. Some forty per cent of the general membership of a typical regional Teckel-klub in Germany own hunting licenses and put their Dachshunds to earth.

In England, too, the deployment of working terriers in the fossorial hunt remains much more common than in the United States. Although the digging out and killing of badgers has been banned in Britain since the passage of the 1973 Badgers Act, the digging out of fox remains a legal and very popular country sport. In March 1998, a proposed Parliamentary bill against Hunting with Dogs prompted a protest by a quarter-of-a-million rural marchers who converged on London's Hyde Park for the Countryside Rally in defense of country blood sports. The Fox Terrier is the mainstay of the underground endgame of the modern English foxhunt.

Although the Fox Terrier is mechanically the best

---

* Australian Terrier, Bedlington Terrier, Border Terrier, Cairn Terrier, Dachshund, Dandie Dinmont Terrier, Fox Terrier (Smooth), Fox Terrier (Wire-haired), Jack Russell Terrier, Jagdterrier, Lakeland Terrier, Norfolk Terrier, Norwich Terrier, Patterdale Terrier, Scottish Terrier, Sealyham Terrier, Skye Terrier, Welsh Terrier, and the West Highland White Terrier.

** The 21-breed AKC roster of breeds automatically eligible for Earthdog Tests departs from the AWTA Den Trials roster by including the Manchester Terrier, Miniature Bull Terrrier, Miniature Schnauzer, and Silky Terrier and excluding the Jagdterrier and Patterdale Terrier.

digger in the Terrier Group, the Lakeland Terrier is the best amphibian. As such, the Lakeland terrier is our best modern functional analogue to the medieval *bibarhunt*. For the Lakeland Terrier excels both as an earth-dog and a water-dog. It eagerly follows a fox or otter to earth—often crawling great distances underground, sometimes pressing the quarry in its den for days on end. The Lakeland Terrier shows itself equally able in the water when, as the specialist adjunct to an Otter Hound pack, it undertakes to dislodge an otter from its underwater sanctuary. In its underground work, normal length and straightness of leg prove no hindrance to the Lakeland Terrier. For its water work, normal length of leg is an outright necessity. A short-legged dog simply cannot swim well enough to worry a semiaquatic quarry in the water. We conclude that it is far more likely that the Bavarian *bibarhunt* had legs of normal length than that it was a short-legged precursor of the modern Dachshund, as has been repeatedly proposed in the standard Dachshund literature.

The enthusiasm shown in the Dachshund literature for the beaver-dog as forebear of the modern Dachshund has been kindled not only by the early medieval allusion in the *Lex Bajuviorum* treated above but also by two purported classical allusions. Whereas the medieval allusion was carelessly over-read, we will show that the classical allusions have been flagrantly mis-read.

In his erudite classic, *The Dachshund or Teckel* (1937), Herbert Sanborn asserts that two Greek authors—Xenophon and Arrian—mention a "beaver-dog" whom both describe as "a dachshund-like dog". Much the earlier of the two, Xenophon (*c.* 431-350 BC) led a bucolic life of literary reflection punctuated by foreign adventures of high drama: he was successively a student of Socrates; an Athenian country gentleman and avid sportsman; an essayist; a mercenary general in the service of various potentates in Asia Minor; a well-rewarded pro-Sparta agent; and a military historian, whose most famous production was *Anabasis*. Sometime before 401 BC, when

he set off on the harrowing military expedition that would become the subject of *Anabasis*, Xenophon wrote a treatise entitled *Kynegetikos* ("On Hunting"), in which he mentions by name—*kastoriai kynes*—a particular breed of hunting dog. It is this breed that Sanborn (*ibid.*) holds up as the forebear of the modern Dachshund in both function (going to earth after vermin) and appearance: "Xenophon makes reference to certain beaver-dogs or *kunes kastoriai*, the description of which agrees in general with that of the dachshund, which is itself thought to be identical with the dog known in ancient Germany as the 'bibarhunt'."

The second Greek author whom Sanborn cites as supplying a description of this ancient forerunner of the Dachshund is Arrian. Although Arrianus Flavius (*c.* AD 96-180) was five centuries Xenophon's junior, his curriculum vitae—student of Epictetus (in fact, the only record that has survived of Epictetus' Stoic philosophy is Arrian's class-notes); provincial governor and general in Asia Minor for Emperor Hadrian; and military historian—so curiously paralleled that of Xenophon that Arrian ventured to style himself "Xenophon the Younger". As though to confirm his nominal succession, Arrian penned his own *Anabasis* and *Kynegetikos*, the latter expressly designed as a supplementary update to the text of his revered predecessor—particularly with respect to the Scythian and Libyan breeds of horses and to the Gallic breeds of hounds, none of which were known to Xenophon's Greece. Sanborn (*ibid.*) states: "The Latin [*sic*] writer Arrianus is said to have described a dog which corresponds closely with the dachshund and it seems the Greeks also had a name for it [*kunes kastoriai*]."

Sadly, in a work so fecund of erudition, Sanborn totally misrepresents what both Xenophon and Arrian actually wrote. First, Sanborn incorrectly translates Xenophon's phrase—*kastoriai kynes*—as "beaver-dog". Although *kastoriai* by itself may indeed mean "of the beaver", it has a quite different meaning when compounded with *kynes* ("dog"). The phrase *kastoriai kynes* is actually a synonym for "Laconian hound", arising from the belief that the first Laconian hounds were bred by Castor (*Kastor*). The heavenly twins Castor and Pollux were regarded as the protectors of the hunt, by virtue of having been educated by Chiron and having assisted in the hunt of the Calydonian boar. The literal translation of the phrase *kastoriai kynes* is not "beaver-dog" but "Castor-dog" or "Castorian hound".

Second, Sanborn's assertion that Xenophon's description of the *kunes kastoria*i "agrees in general with that of the dachshund" is out to lunch. In fact, Xenophon identifies the "Castor-dog" as the famous Laconian packhound so prized by the Greek hunting aristocracy for its celerity in coursing and ferocity in rending the swiftest game such as hare and deer. As depicted in Attic vase painting, fleet Laconian hounds with bushy tails and prick ears streak around amphorae on long, fine legs that could scarcely be less dachshund-like. Xenophon actually writes of the Castorian hound in his *Kynegetikos* (as translated by Denison Hull in *Hounds and Hunting in Ancient Greece*, 1964) as follows:

> Hounds and hunting are the invention of the gods Apollo and Artemis. They gave them, honoring Chiron with them for his righteousness...He had as students of the chase... Theseus,...Castor, Polydeuces [Pollux]... Castor and Polydeuces displayed in Greece so much that they learned from Chiron that they became immortal for these skills because of their own renown...There are two kinds of [Laconian] hounds, the Castorians [kastoriai kynes] and the Vulpines. The Castorians have their name because Castor took especial pleasure in the task of keeping them...They must be big...Their heads must be flat-nosed...; ears small, delicate...; front legs short, straight...; ribs not close to the ground but stretching obliquely;...lower legs long, rounded...They will be strong in appearance, nimble, well proportioned, fast running...Let them follow the scent...putting their heads slanting to the ground...and letting their ears droop. Let them go forward to the hare's form...Let them give chase vigorously without relaxing, giving much clamor and baying, all coming together after the hare on every

side. Let them pursue fast and brilliantly, borne along after her in a pack, giving tongue properly again and again...It is better to take the hounds to the mountains often but to the fields less often, for in the mountains it is possible to run cleanly, but in the fields it is not possible on account of the paths.

Sanborn's third error is to ascribe to Arrian a description in Latin of the same breed that was called by the Greeks *kastoriai kynes* and "which corresponds closely with the dachshund." In fact, nowhere in his *Kynegetikos* (written in Greek, incidentally) does Arrian mention the Castorian hound. Arrian describes only two breeds of hound, both Celtic: the *Segusiae* and the *Vertragi*. Neither of these Celtic hounds corresponds any more closely to the modern dachshund than does the Castorian hound, as is clear from the following excerpts from Arrian's *Kynegetikos* (as translated by Hull, *ibid*.):

> Xenophon did not know any breed of hounds like the Celtic in speed...For they are bred so well in body and in spirit that a hare would never escape them unless some difficult ground or concealing wood hindered...Those Celts who do not make a living by hunting dispense with purse-nets and hunt [hare] for the sheer pleasure of it, for there exists a breed of hounds for hunting this way that is no less clever than the Carian or the Cretan breed [both scenthounds], although its appearance is wretched and wild. And these hunt with a clamor and baying...These hounds are called 'Segusiae', getting their name from a Celtic tribe where first...they bred and esteemed them [the Segusiavi lived in the Gallic province that included modern Lyons]...The Segusiae are rough and sorry-looking, and whichever among them are the best bred are the sorriest, so it is popular among the Celts to liken them to people begging by the roadside. For, indeed, they have a pitiful and mournful cry and therefore do not give tongue on the line as if they were furious at the beast but pitifully and entreatingly. Indeed, it seems to me that it would not be worthwhile for anybody to write anything about them. The fast-running Celtic hounds, on the other hand, are called 'Vertragi' in the language of the Celts...because of

their speed [the Celtic word *Vertragus*—compounded of the intensive *ver* and *trag*, 'foot'—means 'greyhound']. The best bred of them are rather good in appearance, both as to their eyes and as to their whole body, their hair, and their skin...a very pleasant sight to a hunting man.

Xenophon and Arrian describe Laconian and Celtic hounds so unlike the dachshund in function and appearance that one is hard pressed to understand how as careful a student of the breed as Sanborn could have conceived any such similarity in the first place. Perhaps the spurious image was lodged in his imagination by a reading of the passage cited above from Shakespeare's *A Midsummer Night's Dream* describing the points of Theseus' Spartan (Laconian) hounds. In a play in which Puck can magically fix on Bottom the head of an ass, no shadows will be offended if the Duke of Athens magically imposes on his Laconian hounds the bodies and voices of sixteenth-century French *bassets à jambes torses*.

Although none of the Laconian or Celtic hounds described by Xenophon or Arrian resemble the dachshund in function or appearance, some medieval legends suggest at least the possibility of a more tenuous and indirect genealogical link. Sir John Buchanan-Jardine (*ibid.*) speculates that the Segusiae may have been crossed with Laconian hounds to produce the hounds reputedly kept by the seventh-century Bishop of Liége, St. Hubert (AD 656-727), patron saint of the chase (the Christian Castor, if you will). From St. Hubert's kennels at the Episcopal See of Liége, legend has it, proceeded the four royal races: the white hounds of St. Louis; the gray hounds of St. Louis; the fawn hounds of Brittany; and the hounds of St. Hubert. From these four races, in legendary turn, proceeded all the true modern hounds—the bloodhound, the harrier, the beagle, the foxhound, and the basset (including the dachshund). Only by such a roundabout and mythic path of descent can the possibility be countenanced that the Laconian and Celtic hounds may have been ancestors of the dachshund.

One fifteenth-century pictorial detail does, however, hint at an association between the legend of St. Hubert and possible precursors of the Dachshund. For the first representation in European art of a decidedly short-legged dog, dating to about 1450, appears in a painting (egg tempera on wood) by Pisanello (1395-1455/6) entitled *The Vision of Saint Eustace* (National Gallery, London). According to his hagiographers, Eustace was a Roman general under Emperor Trajan who was converted to Christianity by a vision that he beheld on a hunting expedition: between the antlers of a stag that he was pursuing on horseback through a wood near Tivoli appeared a radiant crucifix. Two issues came of this miraculous conversion: Eustace and his family were roasted to death inside a brass bull by Imperial edict; and the martyred Eustace became the patron saint of hunters.

Centuries after the death of St. Hubert in AD 727, his medieval hagiographers coopted the whole story of the miraculous conversion of St. Eustace, resetting it in the Forêt de Freyr in the Ardennes. In effect, St. Eustace and St. Hubert became southern and northern versions of the same patron saint: one hunting the Christ-stag in the woods of Tivoli; the other in the forest of Ardennes. St. Hubert—as St. Eustace's Frankish doppelgänger—was thenceforth accorded equal due as patron saint of hunters and hydrophobia victims. Pisanello's *The Vision of Saint Eustace* might, therefore, be equally regarded as a depiction of the vision of Saint Hubert.

In this painting, Pisanello depicts seven hunting dogs gathered about St. Eustace/St. Hubert, who has reined up his horse in amazement at the vision of the Christ-stag before him (a far more benign stag, it might be noted, than the one that appeared to Jerry Dunn in Louisiana). It is apposite to recall that Pisanello was the most skillful and verisimilitudinous animal portraitist of the century. The dog studies in his studio sketch-album—the *Codex Vallardi* (compiled 1415-22, preserved at the Louvre)—are particularly admired today for their grace, facility, and precocious naturalism.

Five of the seven dogs that Pisanello depicts in *The Vision of Saint Eustace* are instantly recognizable as various long-legged greyhound and scenthound types familiar to us still. The remaining two dogs are a queer-looking brace of smallish, decidedly short-legged dogs with long bodies, pendent ears, gay bushy tails, and reddish-brown coats with light-colored leg-feathering. Their legs are straight and commensurate in length to those of the bassets rendered in the illustrations of both Du Fouilloux (*ibid.*, 1560) and Daubenton (*ibid.*, 1758).

Pisanello's short-legged dogs differ radically from these later bassets, however, in their head conformation, which is not at all houndlike but instead rebarbatively piglike—composed of bulging skull, flat upper face, and underslung conical snout. Baxter the weeny dog they are not. In point of fact, they look in the head quite unlike any dogs with which we are familiar today—but very like

that exceedingly odd brace of dogs that figure in the copperplate executed by Ammon (*ibid.*, 1590) to illustrate Du Fouilloux' account of the *charrette de chasse* expedition with bassets to a badger ground.

Pisanello's short-legged dogs pose a conundrum. On the basis of their short-leggedness, they seem to qualify for consideration as the missing morphological link between the Bedford Master's long-legged badger-earth-going *limiers* of the early fifteenth century and Du Fouilloux' short-legged badger-earth-going *bassets* of the middle sixteenth century. On the other hand, their bizarre cranial conformation seems to augur nothing but an evolutionary dead end for Pisanello's short-legged dogs—a barely noticed late medieval breed blanked by oblivion after the sixteenth century. Moreover, nothing in Pisanello's painting indicates that the short-legged dogs are earth-dogs. To the contrary, they are overtly depicted as

engaged in scent-trailing in a stag-chase.

Although Pisanello's painting contains the earliest European image of an emphatically short-legged dog, ancient Egypt produced images of achondroplastic hounds that antedate *The Vision of Saint Eustace* by more than three millennia. The same Dachshund breed enthusiasts who glibly impute short-leggedness to the medieval Bavarian *bibarhunt* and to the classical Greek *kastoriai kynes* could scarcely be expected to exercise restraint when faced with the temptation of appropriating the impressive antiquity of the Egyptian images to the Dachshund breed. In their uncritical effort to roll back the pedigree of the Dachshund to the very dawn of human civilization, such enthusiasts have foisted even wilder and more willful misconstructions upon the Egyptian paleographic record than upon the Greek.

Ilgner (*ibid.*) argues that the modern German Dachshund is directly descended from an ancient Egyptian breed, citing as evidence the representation of a certain dog on a tablet in the Museum of Bulak near Thebes, as reproduced by Vero Shaw in *The Illustrated Book of the Dog* (1881). Ilgner reports that this dog is represented lying at the feet of a King of Egypt; with abnormally short front legs; and labeled with phonemic hieroglyphs that sound the name *Tekal*. From the homophonic similarity between Egyptian *Tekal* and modern German *Teckel*, Ilgner concludes that the modern Dachshund must be descended in name and body from the Egyptian *Tekal* breed.

Unfortunately for his theory, Ilgner got his data all wrong. Samuel Birch—Britain's top Egyptologist in the nineteenth century—published a paper in 1875 dating the limestone tablet in question to the XIIth-dynasty reign of Inyotef II (2065-2016 BC). On the tablet, according to Birch, are painted in profile four dogs of different long-legged breeds, each distinguished by its peculiar collar and hieroglyphic label.

One of the dogs stands between the legs of the Pharoah and bears a hieroglyphic inscription consonantally transcribed as *tkk*, and translated as "attacker". (By Ilgner's free-association etymological method, the English word *attack* obviously derives from ancient Egyptian *tkk*.) As depicted on the tablet, the *tkk* has long, straight legs; a short, deep muzzle; and small, prick ears. A dog more un-dachshund-like in appearance and function could scarcely be imagined. Like the medieval Bavarian *biberhunt* and the classical Greek *kastoriai kynes*, the ancient Egyptian *tkk* must be eliminated from the proto-Dachshund sweepstakes.

Yet a search of the corpus of ancient Egyptian art turns up another painted image which does qualify for consideration as a proto-Dachshund. The archeological site of Beni Hasan consists of 39 rock tombs of XIth- and XIIth-dynasty nome officials cut into limestone cliffs on the east bank of the Nile 155 miles south of Cairo. Some of the tombs are painted with murals of daily life, some of which contain images of dogs of various types. One of these images from the first half of the XIIth dynasty (*c.* 1900 BC) depicts a long-bodied, achondroplastically short-legged, hound-headed, lactescent black-and-tan bitch that looks a lot like a smooth-coated Dachshund.

In *The Dog* (1968), Fernand Mery remarks that this Dachshund-like Egyptian dog must have been a short-lived breed insofar as no representations of it can be found in the art of other dynasties. Mery speculates that the XIIth-dynasty Dachshund-like dog might have been "the result of some unexpected mutation of the greyhound"— the latter being a perennial breed that is figured throughout the history of Egyptian art from the Vth dynasty (2465 BC) onward.

Actually, the idea that the abnormally short-legged Egyptian breed appeared as the result of a spontaneous mutation in a normal breed; that this mutant breed soon went extinct; and that our abnormally short-legged modern breeds result from recurrences of the same spontaneous mutation in modern normal dogs rather than from the continuous transmission of the hereditary mutation down a 4,000-year-long lineage of abnormally short-legged dogs was first proposed exactly a century before Mery. In *The Variation of Animals and Plants under Domestication* (1868), Charles Darwin wrote:

> ...on Egyptian monuments from the 4th to the 12th dynasties...there is...a turnspit, with short and crooked legs, closely resembling the existing variety; but this kind of monstrosity is so common with various animals, as with ancon sheep, and even, according to Rengger, with jaguars in Paraguay, that it would be rash to look at the monumental animal as the parent of our turnspits.

INDEX

achondroplasia in dogs: its micromelic distinguished from its brachycephalic forms, 23; its causes and effects distinguished from those of ateliosis, 24; its simultaneous operation with ateliosis in dogs, 24; its multiple manifestation in certain breeds, 24; independent mandibular and maxillary components of the brachycephalic form of, 24, 27; compared to human achondroplasia, 27, 28, 30; its operation in Dachshunds, 24, 30; its operation in an Ancient Egyptian dog-type, 109

Allan, Jamie ("Piper"), 98

American Kennel Club (AKC): trends in its popularity ranking of the Dachshund, 9; its Dachshund standard, 16, 19; its assignment of the Dachshund to a succession of Groups, 93, 103; its heterogeneous Terrier Group, 103; Earthdog Trials regulated by, 104, 104n

American Working Terrier Association (AWTA): trials of, 104; eligible breeds within, 104n

Ammon, Jost (1539-91), his woodcuts of bassets to illustrate the first German translation of Du Fouilloux, 57

Arrian (Arrianus Flavius) (c. AD 96-180); 105; his description of two Celtic hounds in his *Kynegetikos*, 106-107

badger, Eurasian (*Meles meles*): 10, 13-14; described by Turberville, 53; described by Phébus, 80

badger-dog, early modern: *see* Dachshund; basset; terrier

badger-dog, medieval: its appearance as depicted by the Bedford Master in *Miroir de Phébus*, 85; *see also limier*

badger hunting: described by von Hohberg, 44, 47; described by Du Fouilloux, 47; described by Turberville, 53, 54; described and illustrated in *Miroir de Phébus*, 83, 85; revival in the U.S. since 1971, 103-104; outlawed in Britain by 1973 Badgers Act, 104

basset: its achondroplastic similarity to the Dachshund, 24; its historical identity with the Dachshund, 33-57 passim, 64, 68-69, 87-91, 108; its divergence from the Dachshund in the 19th century, 33-35

beaver (*Castor fiber*), 73

beaver-dog, classical: shown to be spurious, 105-106, 108-109

beaver-dog, medieval (or *bibarhunt*): 71, 73, 74; Lakeland terrier as best modern functional analogue to, 105

beaver-dog, baroque (or *Biberhund*), 44, 74

beaver hunting, 73-74

Bedford, Duke of (1389-1435), 85

Bedford Master (fl 1423-1435), 76, 78, 80, 83, 85

Beni Hasan, site of XIIth-Dynasty tomb mural of Dachshund-like bitch, 109

Bewick, Thomas (1753-1828), 96

Birch, Samuel (1813-1885), his report on dogs painted on XIIth-Dynasty Egyptian tablet, 108-109

Blome, Richard (d. 1705), 93

Boece, Hector (c. 1465-c. 1536), his description of the Scottish sleuth-hound, 95-96

Braun, Eva (1910-1945), her Scottish Terriers, 100

Brown, Thomas (1785-1862), author of the first description of disproportionately short-legged Scottish terriers, 96

Buchanan-Jardine, Sir John William, (Master of Dumfrieshire Foxhounds) (b. 1900): 39; his speculation on descent of St. Hubert hound from classical hound, 107

Buffon, Georges-Louis Leclerc, comte de (1707-1788), 36, 63, 68, 69

Caius, Johannes (1510-1573): author of the first taxonomy of British dogs, 58, 86; his *Terrarius*, 48, 68, 86-87, 88; his *Vertagus*, 66-68; his Turnspit, 68; his Lyemmer, 77

classical dog-types, erroneously adduced as Dachshund forerunners: Laconian (or Castorian or Spartan) hounds, 105-106; Celtic hounds, 106-107

Countryside Rally (London, 1998), in defense of hunting with dogs, 104

Couteulx de Canteleu, le comte le (fl 1863-1890), 35, 90

Cox, Nicholas (1650?-1731), 68, 91, 96

Dachshund: effects of World Wars on national populations of, 7-9; AKC registration trends of, 9; edacious nicknames of, 7, 9, 10, 21; original badger-hunting function of, 10-14, 57; badger-like characteristics of, 13-14; size classes of, 14-16, 103; coat classes of, 16-19, 69, 103; somatype of, 21-23; genotype of, 23-30; compared to basset, 33-57 passim, 64, 68-69, 87-91, 110; compared to Niederlaufhund, Bracke and Schweisshund 41; its evolution, whether independent or radial with respect to other achondroplastic hound breeds, 41-42; 19th-century varieties, 66-69

Dachshund, national breed clubs: *Internationaler Dackel-Club Gergweis e.V.* (IDG), 14, 100-101; *Deutscher Teckelklub e.V.* (DTK), 14-19, 100, 102; Dachshund Club of Great Britain (DC), 16, 100; Dachshund Club of America (DCA), 16, 102; priority of British institutions, 100; the fissile effects of, comparable to those affecting Scottish terriers, 93, 101-102

DC (Dachshund Club of Great Britain) *see* Dachshund, national breed clubs

DCA (Dachshund Club of America) *see* Dachshund, national breed clubs

Dachshund, inappropriate Linnaean binomial for: 60, 66, 66-69, 86, 106-107

Dachshund, the word: its literal meaning, 10; its earliest attested occurrences, 33, 42-44, 58; its German synonyms: *Teckel, Dackel, Dachel, Dachsel*, 10; *Schlieffer, Schlieff-Hündlein, kleine Schlieffhund, Tachs Schlieffer*, 44, 60; *Dachsfinder*, 44; *Dachs kriecher, Tachs kriecher*, 57, 58, 60

Dachshund owners, notable: 9, 60, 100

Dachshunds, notable: 10, 60

Dandie Dinmont (terrier breed), 16, 97-98, 100, 101

Daniel, William Barker (1753-1833), 93

Darwin, Charles (1809-1882): on artificial selection for achondroplasia in bulldogs and turnspits, 23; rejects notion of hereditary descent of modern turnspit from Ancient Egyptian turnspit, 109

Daubenton, Louis-Jean-Marie (1716-1800), 35, 36, 39, 63-64, 66, 108

Davidson, James (developer of "Dandie Dinmont" strain), 97-98, 100

Deutsche Jagdterrier, developed from British terriers as substitute for Dachshund, 100, 104n

Dinmont, Dandie (character in *Guy Mannering*), *see* Davidson, James

Döbel, H.W., 33, 63

Dorfmeister, Kathi (IDG foundress), 101

DTK (*Deutscher Teckelklub e.V.*) *see* Dachshund, national breed clubs

Du Fouilloux, Jacques (1521-80): 33, 35, 36, 44, 47, 85, 87, 88, 90, 96, 104, 108; woodcuts in his *La Vénerie* depicting *bassets*, 47-48; his text on badger dogs and hunting, 48-57; his description of the *limier*, 77

Edward, Duke of York (1373-1415), 78

Edwards, Sydenham Teast (1769-1819), 96

Elizabethan dog-types, non-earthdog: lyemmer, 77, 86;

111